DISCARD

TWO YEARS' EXPERIENCE
AMONG
THE SHAKERS

DAVID R. LAMSON

AMS PRESS
NEW YORK

MOUNTAIN MEETING.—See page 56.

TWO YEARS' EXPERIENCE

AMONG

THE SHAKERS:

BEING A DESCRIPTION OF THE

Manners and Customs of that People,

THE NATURE AND POLICY OF THEIR GOVERNMENT,

Their Marvellous Intercourse with the Spiritual World,

THE OBJECT AND USES OF CONFESSION,

THEIR INQUISITION,

IN SHORT, A CONDENSED VIEW OF

SHAKERISM AS IT IS.

By DAVID R. LAMSON.

"There is nothing covered, that shall not be revealed; neither hid, that shall not be known." — JESUS CHRIST.

WEST BOYLSTON:
PUBLISHED BY THE AUTHOR.
1848.

BX 9773
.L3
1971

Reprinted from the edition of 1848: West Boylston

First AMS edition published in 1971

Manufactured in the United States of America

International Standard Book Number: 0-404-08477-X

Library of Congress Catalog Card Number: 71-134418

AMS PRESS INC.
NEW YORK, N.Y. 10003

PREFACE.

The following pages have been prepared with the view of throwing light upon the subject of Shakerism. The Shakers being a very secret as well as very singular people, very little can be known of their internal affairs and mysteries, except by those who have lived among them. And even the common members have little or no correct knowledge of the real policy of their government, or the origin of the mysteries they behold, and at which they marvel. The objectionable parts of the system are carefully kept from the view of visiters, and from their neighbors; and from those who join them from the world as long as practicable.

Many people in the world, viewing only the smiling and peaceful exterior of Shakerism, have a longing wish to be connected with them, feeling that by so doing, they shall release themselves from the care and turmoil of life. But a very short experience, in almost every case, suffices them, and they withdraw. This is a costly and vexatious way of obtaining a knowledge of Shakerism; and to remove the necessity of such a course, is a principal object of this work.

The works which have preceded this on the same subject, if not true in every particular, yet contain much more truth than I could believe prior to my experience among that people. They contain some things which my own experience among that people does not enable me to confirm ; yet as the authors of those works may have gone deeper into the hidden things of that kingdom than I was able to do, I do not feel warranted in saying they are untrue.

I have made no statements in the following work which I do not know or fully believe to be true, and can substantiate by indubitable evidence.

It may not be improper to state also, that I have written with no ill feelings, or desire to injure that people. But on the principle that the public have a right to the facts developed in this work, and to comply with the numerous solicitations I have received for such a work. Personally, I was treated by the Shakers with great kindness and consideration ; and during the sickness of my children, no efforts seemed to be spared on their part to render them comfortable, and procure their recovery. I take great pleasure in acknowledging this goodness of theirs, and most heartily reciprocate all their good feelings. And still feel a duty in exposing the whole truth.

Doubtless the "Lead" will do as they have done in regard to other works on this subject: viz. use all the means in their power to prevent their subjects from reading it. Such is the policy of their government, and is necessary to their continuance as a people. D. R. L.

INDEX.

Compendium of the History of Shakerism,	9
Description of the village,—its name,	15
Reasons for going to the Shakers,	'8
Their Government,	27
How the authority of the "Lead" is supported,	30
Birth day of Mother Ann, and the Holy Laws,	32
The manner of taking their meals,	42
Education,	46
Communion with the spiritual world,	50
Ceremony of anointing,	50
Family meetings, a description of,	52
Mountain meetings—the ground, fountain, monument,	56
Heavenly Dress for the occasion,	58
Written revelations given on the mountain,	73
Gifts, songs, unknown tongues,	78
Whirling gift,	85
David Terry's gifts, warring gifts,	88
Gift of Holy Mother Wisdom,	93
The Father and the Son,	97
Cleansing gift and roaring song,	105
A revelation concerning the personality of the devil,	107
Annual fast,	109
Sacred Roll and Book,	111
Extracts from the Second part,	129
Testifying seal of the prophet Jeremiah,	129
The prophet Elisha,	130
Testimony of the Eleven Angels,	130
" " Harriet Goodwin,	133
" " Martha Van Vaiin,	143
" " Adah Zillah Potter,	146
" " Joseph Wicker,	148
" " Mary Ann Jennings, and a seal from the Lord Jehovah,	149
" " Benjamin Seth Youngs,	154
Remarks,	156
Gifts of healing, a miracle,	159
Confession of sins,	164
Community of property,	169
A plan for those who would throw off the yoke,	173
Keeping children against the wish of parents,	174
Case of Robert Jenkins' children, and petition to the Lodge of Odd Fellows,	177
Manner of treating those who wish to leave them,	184
Case of Jane Ann Weed,	185
Story of Mary Williams and William Wright,	193
Are the "Lead" pure from the sin of carnality?	196
Foundlings,	200
Principal doctrines.—Second Advent,	201
Do the "Lead" believe in the pretended revelations?	206
Community of property. Conclusion.	207

A COMPENDIUM

OF THE

HISTORY OF SHAKERISM.

Ann Lee was the founder of the Society called *Shakers*. She was born in Manchester, England, Feb. 29, 1736. Her father was a blacksmith, a poor man with a large family. Ann was married to Abraham Stanley, who had served his apprenticeship with her father, before she was 18 years of age. By him she had four children. Three of them died in infancy; the other at the age of six years.— After embracing the doctrine of celibacy she was separated from her husband, and resumed her maiden name. He joined himself to another woman.

When it is said that Ann Lee was the founder of Shakerism, the statement requires some qualification. She did not originate the whole system. Many of its peculiarities may be traced back nearly two hundred years, to a remarkable religious revival which took place in France, among the protestants, or, as they were then called, "Huguenots," who were then much persecuted by the Catholics. Great numbers of the subjects of this revival, made pretensions to very extraordinary and supernatural inspirations. They pretended to be endowed with all the apostolic gifts:— prophesying, healing, raising from the dead, speaking in unknown tongues, falling in trances, trembling, shaking, having various spasms or agitations of the body, &c. These are known by the appellation of "The French

HISTORY OF SHAKERISM.

Prophets." They were of both sexes, and of all ages, from six years old and upwards. This revival occured about the year 1668. Many of these fled to England to escape persecution.

In 1747 these peculiarities were revived in England by James Wardley and his wife, Jane, and others, who organized themselves into a society. These were principally from the denomination of Quakers, and therefore they were, at first, called Shaking Quakers. Matrimony was allowed among them at this time. They held the doctrine of the confession of sins. And Jane Wardley was called Mother by the other members of the society.

Ann Lee joined this society in 1758, being in her 23rd year of age. By her zeal and energy she gained considerable influence in the society, and the aged "Lead," James and Jane Wardley, finally resigned their office in her favor. The apostolic gifts to which Shakers now pretend, the various agitations of the body, the confession of sins, the idea of a Spiritual Mother, &c., doubtless originated with the French prophets, and have been handed down to the present day. But the doctrine of total-abstinence from sexual coition, their doctrine of the second Advent, the organization and government of their society, originated with "Mother Ann and the elders with her."

She, and those of her followers whose circumstances enabled them to do so, emigrated to America in 1774. The names of those who came with her were Abraham Stanley, (her husband) Wm. Lee, her brother, Nancy Lee, her neice, Mary Partington, James Whitaker, John Hocknell, and James Shepherd. J. Shepherd and A. Stanley, afterwards withdrew from them. The remaining six established Shakerism in America. They arrived in New York on the 6th of August. Soon after, by the advice of some benevolent Quakers, they proceeded up the North river to Watervliet, then called Niskeyund; here they purchased the spot where they have maintained a society to the present day.

John Hocknell was the only one among them at this time who was possessed of any considerable amount of

HISTORY OF SHAKERISM. 11

property; and to his property the society is indebted for its infantile support. After purchasing at Watervleit, they returned to New York, and Hocknell returned to England for his family. During the absence of Hocknell the other members were employed at their various occupations. Ann and her husband in New York, Wm. Lee, Shepherd and Whitaker, in Albany. Hocknell returned in Dec. 1775, accompanied by his family, and John Partington and family. The ensuing Spring, the working members of the society repaired to Watervleit and laid the foundation of their settlement, where the other members joined them in the Autumn of 1776. Here they remained in obscurity for the space of three or four years, when an opening was made for their efforts by means of a remarkable revival in New Lebanon, N. Y., then called Canaan. To this place the Mother and elders repaired, and were successful in making proselytes. In this place they now have their largest and most efficient society. Here is the residence of the supreme pontiff. This place is called the "Head of influence and centre of union."

Their success at New Lebanon encouraged the Shakers to extend their labors. Ann and the elders travelled and labored wherever any encouragement was held out to them. They succeeded in establishing meetings in Hancock, Harvard in Mass. and several other places within a few years.

In 1780, being the days of the American Revolution, Ann Lee, and those of her followers at Watervleit, from some circumstances, were suspected of treason. And she, with nine of her most influential men, were arrested and imprisoned at Poughkeepsie; some were also imprisoned at Albany. Governor Clinton, as soon as he learned these facts, ordered their release. This persecution rather favored, than hindered the Shakers in their success. The Mother and elders were indefatigable in their endeavors to spread their views and peculiarities; and, by their zeal and perseverance, they succeeded in establishing societies in various parts of the country. But the people were not brought into order, as they expressed it, until after the death of Mother Ann.

HISTORY OF SHAKERISM.

During her life in America she was supported by her elders, James Whitaker, William Lee, and John Hocknell. And doubtless, the greater part of the credit for the success of Shakerism, is due them rather than her. She doubtless originated the doctrine of celibacy. But the idea of her being the second appearance of Christ, was urged upon her by her cabinet of elders. They were doubtless efficient and practical men.

The character given Ann Lee by history, is, that she was a woman of good natural abilities, but extremely illiterate. Possessed of strong feelings, a powerful imagination, and a high temper. She is represented as having been intemperate in the use of alcoholic liquors. Some who were cotemporary with her have testified that they have seen her come to hard blows with elder Wm. Lee—have seen her much intoxicated. And that she was in the habit of using profane and obscene language. The Shakers now deny these accusations as a matter of course; as well as many other things brought against her moral character, and sustained by pretty good authority. She died on the 8th of Sept. 1784—having appointed James Whitaker to be her successor in the pontificate.

Elder William Lee died a few months previous to the death of Ann. He is represented as a man of great personal beauty, and great personal strength. And while in England, as well skilled and practiced in the pugilistic art. He is represented as very illiterate, rough in his manners, and not very successful as a preacher. He died July 21, 1784.

James Whitaker succeeded Ann Lee in office, which he held from 1784 to 1786, when he died—having appointed Joseph Meacham his successor. He was succeeded at his death and by his appointment, by Lucy Wright, called Mother Lucy. Joseph Meacham reigned from 1786 to 1796. Lucy Wright from 1796 to 1821, when she died—having appointed, as her successor, Ebenezer Bishop, who yet holds the office in 1848. Lucy Wright, before joining the Shakers, was married to E. Goodrich, with whom she lived for a considerable time.

Joseph Meacham, during the term of his office, disposed the Shakers into their present *orders*, and *families*. He was, therefore, the author of their present peculiar organization, and gave them their covenant by which they hold their community property. He was the first native American who filled the office of Shaker Pontiff. Previous to joining this people he was a preacher of the Baptist denomination. And to his learning and natural abilities is Shakerism indebted for its present order and stability.

About the year 1801 there commenced a remarkable religious revival in Kentucky, to which the Shakers are indebted for a large increase to their denomination. Their societies in the Western states are the fruits they gathered from this revival. They have recently had some accessions from the Millerites, or Second Advent brethren. But probably these accessions will not be very permanent.

The number of members in this denomination of christians cannot, at the present time, be very definitely ascertained. It is manifestly the policy of the "Lead" to keep the matter a secret, not only from the world, but also from the lay members in the denomination. The secessions in the several societies are kept as secret as possible from the lay members of the other societies. It would doubtless be considered a great sin for any "David to number their Israel" at the present time. And some heavy calamities to them might be the consequence of such a proceeding.

They have been variously estimated from 4000 to 6000. But are supposed to have considerably diminished within the last 15 or 20 years. I perceive that in former estimates the society at Hancock is set down at 300. At the present time, it will not far exceed 150, exclusive of about 30 children who have recently been indentured to them by their parents and guardians. A very large proportion of these members are aged, and already superannuated. If the other societies have decreased in the same proportion, the denomination cannot, at the present time, number over 2500 members. Probably, in their most flourishing condition, they did not exceed 5000 members. Secessions are frequent in all their societies. And for many years their accessions have been few. The children whom they take pains to educate in the way of Shakerism generally leave them soon after they attain their majority. As a denomination they are manifestly on the decrease. It is my opinion that at the present time, they cannot exceed 3000 members. These are scattered over the United States in 17 distinct societies. These all receive their laws and government from the supreme elder at New Lebanon, N. Y. There are two societies in Kentucky, two in Ohio, three in New York, one in Connecticut, four in Massachusetts, two in New Hampshire, two in Maine, and one in Indiana.

By means of their organization and covenant, all the property is consecrated to the purposes of the society. So that seceders can carry nothing away with them. Therefore their property does not diminish with the diminution of their members. The less their number the greater their wealth. As their numbers diminish, however, their large farms somewhat lessen in value for the want of better cultivation.

Their most important and distinguishing doctrines are, first, that Christ has made his second appearance in Ann Lee, and that now is the Millennium. Second, the doctrine of the " Cross," or entire abstinence from sexual coition. In connexion with this they teach that " *all natural affections*" must be subdued and put away. We must have no affection for natural relations, except they belong to the church, in which case they may be regarded as other christians. Third, that the days of miracles and revelations are not passed; but are enjoyed and exercised in their church as fully as in the days of the apostles. Fourth, that there are two persons in the Godhead of the Deity, male and female.—" The Father, and Holy Mother Wisdom." These have manifested themselves on earth through Jesus Christ, the Son; and Ann Lee, the Daughter. These last are the Two Anointed Ones; the Savior of mankind.

Note.—Whatever of importance may be omitted in this compend of Shaker history will be found supplied in the body of the work.

TWO YEARS AMONG THE SHAKERS.

In the spring of 1843, the year memorable for the great Miller excitement; the year when "The heavens should pass away with a great noise, and the elements melt with fervent heat, the earth also, and the works therein, be burnt up;" although now 1847, the fields are as green, the sun as bright, the birds as gay, and all nature as lovely as ever; this spring of —43, found me and mine, a wife and two little children, most pleasantly and happily associated with that singular and mysterious people, the *Shakers*, in that neat, orderly and sober little village, called by its occupants "the city of Peace." The domain of this little community, or rather this branch of a larger community, extends from the western boundary of Massachusetts easterly, embracing the southern portion of the town of Hancock, a portion of Pittsfield on the east, and of Richmond on the south. Which together with isolated farms which they own in the vicinity, amounts probably to five or six thousand acres. The mountainous parts are well wooded, with beach, maple, and hickory. The lower lands consist of those beautiful swells or undulations which are always productive, including a considerable extent of bottom lands, which make very valuable natural mowing.

Here we find large stocks of excellent cattle, horses, sheep and swine. In having a large and valuable domain well stocked, this society is not singular. It is so in all the societies of this denomination. As a people they are rich in this world's goods.

The village of this society is situated near the centre of their domain. It consists of six large dwelling houses with their out houses, shops, mills, &c. One church and the ministry's shops. Their houses are not close to each other, but generally about a half mile distant. The society being divided into families and orders, in the centre is the church family, or first order. Their house is of brick, 40 feet by 80, three stories high exclusive of basement and attick. Roofed with tin, and finished outside and inside in the most perfect though plain manner. It ends to the road which runs east and west. The house is mounted with a small belfry, the bell of which rings the early hour of rising, and calls the brethren and sisters to their frugal meals. On the east of the house is a large yard with level walks laid with flagstone. On your right as you walk east, is the large round barn. It is a curiosity and a good model for those who have large farms. There are also some other out buildings on the right and on the left as you pass on, at a sufficient distance apart to have an ample and pleasant yard. At the east end of this yard is the trustees office, kept by two brothers and two sisters, where all visiters must call. Here also is a dwelling house and other buildings convenient for a large family. On the west of the main dwelling of the church family house are also several buildings; three houses, each sufficiently capacious for an ordinary family. One is designated as the sisters' workshop; where their sewing, and some of their spinning and weaving are done. Of the other two, one is the brethren's nurse shop, and the other the sisters' nurse shop, where the sick are nursed and tended. A little to the south of this is a large building called the machine shop. It has a water power, the water for which is brought from a pond about half a mile distant, in a cast iron aqueduct. Opposite the main building and across the road is the meeting house, on the lower floor of which the several families (except the church order) generally hold one meeting on each Sabbath. The upper story is the dwelling-house of the ministry; (two men and two women.) This is considered a very sacred place. In "the holy laws" it is forbidden that any one should enter the dwelling of the holy ministry. At the east of this are two buildings, two stories high each. These are the ministry's work-shops. One for the two brethren, and the other for the two sisters. If the elders have any business with the ministry, they may call at their shops. These constitute the principal buildings of a single family, including their office and the buildings belonging with it, the ministry's dwelling and work-shops. Quite a village of itself.

Besides this, there are five other families, each having large and commodious buildings. The direction of these from the church family, two east, a quarter and a half mile distant. One south, one west, one north. Generally designated by their direction from the church family, (except the nearest, which is called the 2d family) as the east family, south-house, north-house, and west family. The church family and north-house compose the first order; the 2d family and west family the 2d order; the east family and south-house the 3d or gathering order.

This society consists of about two hundred people in all; a large proportion of which are superannuated, and from 30 to 40 children recently taken in. The efficient laborers in the society are few. Their buildings would accommodate I should judge, a thousand as well as ordinary families are accommodated. And their lands and shops would afford employment for these, provided more than half of them were efficient laborers.

This people are strict utilitarians. In all they do, the first inquiry is, "will it be useful?" Every thing therefore about their buildings, fences, &c., is plain. Their buildings were made capacious with a view to receive the world when they shall be converted to shakerism. Although every thing is plain, there is about the whole village an air of plenty, neatness and comfort which gives it the appearance of a little paradise as it were. And then the singular dress, the mysterious and exclusive manners of the people give them at first sight almost the appearance of a different order of beings. Their high pretensions to purity and goodness together with their singularities is admirably calculated to captivate a stranger ; especially if a little enthusiastic on religious subjects, and withall a little disgusted with the popular religions of the world.

It should be borne in mind by the reader throughout this work, that whatever is described of one family or society of Shakers, in which they differ from the world at large, is equally applicable to every other family or society. It is a description of the denomination. There is an almost perfect uniformity among them, of dress, language, manners, forms of worship, government, &c.

In March of 1843, I visited this little earthly paradise in search of the people of God. It was the first time I had ever seen a Shaker in Shaker habiliments. I had heard of the people, and had heard many contradictory accounts of them. Some of which were very favorable, others very detrimental to them. They made the highest professions of being the only people of God. Considering all others of every persuasion as being in the lowest depths of carnality and sin.

My friends have often asked, "Why ? How came you to go to the Shakers? I always told them (that is, our friends) you would not stay long."—Their prediction proved true in part; though based more on conjecture than actual knowledge. But I will endeavor to tell as briefly as possible why I went there. And the sequel of of my story will tell why I came away. I professed to be a disciple of Jesus Christ. And therefore I sympathised with, and advocated every good work of the day. As "*moral reform*," temperance, abolition, peace, &c. It did not seem to me possible that there could be a greater inconsistency than for one to profess Christianity, and yet be opposed to these reforms. They were to me vital. But the church, as a body, the nominal church, was the enemy of reform. I looked to its past history, and found that the popular and reigning religionists of the day in which they lived have been, in all ages, as they were now the enemies of moral reform. It was the orthodox church of the Jews who stoned and killed the true prophets of

God, and finally murdered his only begotten son. And afterwards, when the sect of Christians became powerful, they also became corrupt, and under "Constantine the great," (for he shed much blood and was therefore called great;) all who presumed to differ from "the church," that is, all reformers, were put to death. And afterwards, what horrors and atrocities were enacted by the Catholic Inquisition! When these things were done, Catholicism was the orthodoxy of the day. And its victims were the reformers of the day. They were those who dared to speak against its corruptions and abominations. Even so in these latter days. A McDowal is persecuted unto death by the all powerful church and clergy, for his advocacy of an unpopular reform. Temperance lecturers have every where been beaten with brickbats and rotten eggs; not directly by the church as a body; but in the early days of temperance, it was a sort of second hand application of the opinion and influence of the church upon this subject. From the same influence also in 1837, I think it was, every church in the City of Boston, was refused the "New England Anti-Slavery Convention, to celebrate its anniversary in. And afterwards Wm. Loyd Garrison was dragged through the streets of Boston with a halter around his neck, by a mob, composed of men of "property and standing." The testimony of the leading Abolitionists is, that "the church and clergy are the great bulwark of American slavery." So also in regard to the subject of peace. It is a truth too palpable to require proof that the nominal church, both Catholic and Protestant, is a war-making church. Its members learn the art of war, and compose the militia;—our army and navy. Had the church, as a body, been opposed to war, our war with Mexico could not have existed. Here then are the great vices of the age in which we live. War, slavery, intemperance and licentiousness. And what evil is there which befalls mankind, that does not have its origin in one of these? In them we find the source of all mischief and misery, to the human race. And yet every combination which has been formed for their removal has been regarded as more or less hostile to the church.

I had the honor to be acknowledged as a minister of the gospel, and was duly appointed in charge of a church and society. But because I boldly denounced intemperance and slavery as sins to be repented of, I became unpopular, was not countenanced by my brethren in the ministry, and lost my position. And now stand in the same relation to the church as all true and faithful reformers stand. And was greatly disgusted with the empty professions and formalities of the members of the nominal church. Yet the Christianity of Christ was to me every thing, and I believed there must be somewhere on earth the true and visible church.

Having found a few persons who sympathized with me, we organized ourselves into a church, and solemnly, and publicly declared our sentiments in favor of the great reforms of the day, temperance, abolition, peace, chastity, and other moral and religious duties. And on this foundation we formed the community at Hopedale.

But here also I was destined to be disappointed. In about six months from the time we began to assemble at Hopedale the constitution of our society underwent a radical change. The industrial organization, and equality of wages were abandoned. The community of interest given up, and the interest paid on the capital stock before wages were paid for labor. Also their obligation to support their own poor was stricken out of the compact, and an article inserted which provided that they should be supported by "*voluntary* contribution." Of course, if none volunteered their support, it must come from another quarter. This alteration was effected by a minority whose power, (though they were not rich) was their money. The president and Ebenezer D. Draper were the principal advocates for this change. The prevailing argument was, that if the change was not made, they should withdraw themselves and their capital stock. The majority feeling too poor to do without this last; generously withdrew from the council, and allowed the minority to do their own work, according to their own mind. My opposition to this alteration, and to some of the preliminaries of the same character, begat a jealousy in the president towards me and lost me his friendship.

A few days after this work was done, he came to me privately, and generously requested me to withdraw from the community. I did not see fit to comply, did not resign my membership; but as it was not convenient for the community to employ all its members to advantage, or accommodate them with house room, I removed my family and employed myself out of the community. Thinking that perhaps I might sometime return again. But in my short experience there, I had been greatly disappointed; I began to think there must be a people somewhere better even than this fraternal communion.

Being now thoroughly disgusted with the popular religion of the day, and finding in it no tendency to reform the prevailing vices of the age, I began to inquire if there was any thing better.—If there was any society or denomination which practiced in a tolerable degree the spirit and principles of Christianity. For it did and does seem to me, (and I say it in humility and in great deference to public sentiment,) that the great mass of professors of religion, and the leading influence of the church, are radically deficient in the very thing they profess to have obtained.

Having heard much of the Shakers, both good and bad, and hoping the good was true, and the bad false; I determined to make them a visit. Here I found every thing to all human appearance, neat, plentiful, orderly, peaceful, devout and beautiful. As a people they appeared to be temperate, frugal, industrious, honest and simple hearted. And the great majority of them (to say the least) *are* all this. They acknowledge no allegiance to human government, and have no connection with slavery or war. And as to the licentiousness of the flesh, this blight and mildew of the moral world, of this they seemed wholly pure. Total abstinence from all fleshly indulgence was with them a fundamental doctrine,—the burden of their preaching and their "*daily cross.*" This was always magnified by them as "*the cross.*" Why then, might not these prove to be what they seemed to be, the true people of God?—the only true practical believers in Christianity? And might not this be the only way in which this great sin and enemy of human happiness, could be removed? And if so, then every true man would be willing to sacrifice his natural inclinations and take up his daily cross against the flesh.

In view of all these things, was it unreasonable that I should wish to know more of Shakerism? True, in conversation with the elders, I found some things which damped my hopes a little; they thought too much learning a dangerous and hurtful thing. Educated people were not apt to make good Shakers. Some of their doctrines seemed to me to be gross superstitions. But as I was not obliged to receive these, was not required to subscribe to any creed; I desired to be received on probation. But concluded first to bring my family to visit them. We remained a week, and concluded to connect ourselves with them as members. The only door of entrance was the confession of sins. None can remain there on any other condition. When I inquired of the elder what was necessary for me to do in order to become a member, he told me this was the door; if I confessed my sins and conformed to their orders and regulations, and believed it a duty to take up my cross against the flesh, it was all; and after I had opened my mind to the elder I was called brother. He taught me that it was not necessary to sign the covenant even. That many of their members never had, and probably never would sign it. If after one had traveled in this way for a season, and still desired to make some greater sacrifice, they were permitted to sign the covenant. But I found afterwards that the signing the covenant was a matter of greater importance either to the society or to the individual signing it. If the individual have property, by signing the covenants, he consecrates it to the society forever. It goes in with the common property and he can never reclaim it. If the individual be poor, he still becomes, by signing the covenant, entitled to all the rights, privileges, and immunities, of every other member. But if the member do not sign the covenant and becomes helpless, the society may cast him off. This is sometimes done. A young Irishman by the name of Michael, (I have forgotten the sirname,) came and joined them in the usual way, and worked for them the greater part of one summer while I was there. He lived at the "south-house," as they belonged to the gathering order. Sometime in the latter part of summer he had a turn of ill health and was actually insane. They employed the physician from Richmond, whose opinion was that the young man could never be wholly cured of insanity. They lost no time, but went immediately and cast him upon the town as a pauper; and thus got rid of him. If they wish to get rid of a member however, they most always succeed in some way, whether he has signed the covenant or not. But they have full power to rid themselves of those who have not signed the covenant. It is their policy to get those to sign the covenant who have property, or whose labor will be profitable; for by so doing both property and the labor are consecrated to the good of the society, and can never be reclaimed. I was never therefore a member of the Shaker fraternity in the strictest sense, never having signed the covenant. And this is the case with many who are there, as the elder told me; who, as I was, are treated as equal brethren, and perhaps always will be.

Being a young "believer," as the Shakers term those who have recently come among them, I was allowed yet to hold a correspondence with my friends, and was especially encouraged to hold a discussion with my brethren at Hopedale, through the columns of the "Practical Christian." My second communication to the paper on the subject of our discussion, containing some truths which *the editor* was unwilling should come before its readers, I was summarily shut out from its columns. This I regarded as rather unfair, inasmuch as I had advanced nothing inconsistent with the doctrines or principles of the community; and having done something towards establishing that paper, I felt that I had as good, if not as great a right to its columns as the editor himself. But having the power to thrust me out of its columns, he did not hesitate to do it.

Not long after this we received the following letter of excommunication:

"HOPEDALE, Oct. 16th, 1843.
At a regular meeting of Fraternal Community, No. 1, holden at Hopedale, Oct. 16th, 1843, the following resolutions were passed.

Whereas, David R. Lamson and his wife Mary Lamson, have, at various times and places, expressed their disfellowship with this community, and have united themselves with the people called Shakers; and whereas it has been signified to them that a resignation of their membership with us was a plain dictate of *honesty*, justice, and consistency, which resignation though written months since and even read to private friends, as we are credibly informed, has never been tendered to us, therefore resolved that the said David R. Lamson, and Mary Lamson, cannot rightfully be considered any longer members of this community.

Resolved that the secretary of this community be instructed forthwith to communicate a letter containing a copy of these resolutions to the said David R. Lamson, and Mary, his wife.

The above is a true copy of the resolutions passed.
ABBY H. PRICE, *Secretary.*

The 13th article of the Constitution of this community read thus.

" All matters of serious controversy, arising in any community of this association, shall be tried and determined, *in the first instance*, by a mutual council, and upon failure thereof, *finally*, by a jury of twelve impartial members."

But in the haste to get rid of us, the constitutionality of the thing was disregarded. They did not deign to give us any notice even of their intention. Our expulsion was as summary, as it was unconstitutional. There are three distinct charges in the indictment, and, had we been allowed a trial, we should have plead to the first charge, viz. " That we had, at various times and places, expressed our disfellowship with the community." NOT GUILTY. We had doubtless expressed sometime, disapprobation of some of the acts of the community; but this could not rightly be considered an expression of disfellowship of the community. To the 2d charge, viz., that we had " connected ourselves with the Shakers," we should say, guilty in part. We were with this people on a sort of probation ; we had not signed their covenant. And inasmuch as there was not room or employment for us at Hopedale for the time being, what crime was it for us to live with the people of our choice until the way should open for us to return to Hopedale, or determine to remain where we were? It was a place to learn the practical effects of communityism, and I could see no crime in it. To the 3d charge, viz., " that our resignation had been written for months and even read to private friends," we should have plead *guilty*. We had thought of resigning and had consulted our friends on the subject. What wrong did we do the community by this? what law did we trangress, or what right infringe?

But it had been signified to us that we ought to resign. But by whom? not by the community certainly. And if an individual signified any such thing to us, it is to be presumed that he did it on his own authority, and it should be so regarded.

To what then do all these grave charges in this bull of excommunication amount? 1st. I had presumed to disapprove and oppose some of the acts of the society; this was construed into disfellowship, and my wife and self ought to be excommunicated. 2d. It not being convenient for us, or the community, that we should be at Hopedale for the time being, we took up our residence among the people called Shakers ; and, therefore ought to be excommunicated. 3d. We had presumed to think of withdrawing from the community at Hopedale, as we had been invited to do by its president, and had consulted our friends about it, months gone by ; therefore we ought to be excommunicated. 4th. The president had suggested to me that I ought to withdraw ; I remember the suggestion, and my reply was, " I thought, if I withdrew, as a matter of simple right, I should be allowed to explain to my friends, and the friends of the community, through the Practical Christian, the reasons of my withdrawal." But this poor privilege could not be granted me. But the terrible thunder of excommunication was sent forth, and we were annihilated. And the mysteries of Hopedale were not exposed. But the grand argument by which the preamble and resolutions were carried; the idea was a great one; and deep, O how deep must have been the thought which originated it! I know not from what particular mind it emanated, but it came from Hopedale. It was this, "they have withdrawn their joint stock from the community; they may spend it, become poor, and return upon us to be maintained." The resolutions were passed. Though even now, after this mighty reasoning, there were some I am told who did not lift up their hands against us. But these were a few individuals whose charity was not the charity of the community. We were thrust out, and do hereby acknowledge ourselves to be no longer of that church, or that society. And be it known unto all men by these presents, that the fraternal community, No. 1, at Hopedale, have by a bold and summary act, forever freed themselves from all obligations, to support either "voluntarily" or involuntarily, David R. Lamson, or his wife Mary Lamson, or any of their descendants.

So now we are fully at liberty again to look out for ourselves, go where and when we please; we are a part of this wicked world. And if we become too poor to live otherwise, must depend upon its cold charities for the calls of nature.

I ought to apologize to the reader for having introduced this subject into this work at all. But I experienced this affliction, or punishment, from Hopedale, while at the Shakers. My disappointment at Hopedale was one reason of my going to the Shakers. And I have had no means, or opportunity of defending myself against the charges and accusations of the fraternal community. Therefore I have introduced it here, and hope the reader will excuse the same. And I will proceed immediately to the unfolding of Shakerism.

In writing of this people and their *ism*, I have no motive or intention to exaggerate or color any thing. While among them we were treated with more consideration than they usually treat " young believers." Indeed they treated us with great kindness; and much greater liberality than their government allows when strictly adhered to. I was allowed to associate freely with my wife and children, and we were permitted to visit our friends together after we had been with them awhile, without the attendance of a third person. Though this is strictly contrary to their ' holy laws,' we had the permission of the ' holy ministry,' who are above the laws.

Every thing relating to this people is so singular and so curious, that it must, on that account, be interesting to all who love to reflect on religious subjects. It is so full of the marvellous, and has such a commingling of the sublime with the ridiculous. But on another account especially, is it important this subject should be laid open. It is a most crafty game played by the few at the expense of the many. The ministry, elders, and some of the more intelligent and favored of the members, understand well their part. The remainder are kept as ignorant as possible; and by means of the grossest superstition are made to render the most implicit and servile obedience " to their leader." They are most thoroughly enslaved.

The Government.

The government is a perfect despotism. The supreme authority being vested in one individual. It is a very curious anomaly, that a despotism should exist in the midst of a republic. But so it is. The laws of the Shaker Pontiff (or elder as he is called,) are regarded and obeyed as coming directly from Jehovah. The seat of government is at New Lebanon, Columbia co., N. Y. Here emanate all the laws and orders for the several societies throughout the land or world. By all true Shakers these are implicitly and devoutly obeyed; and all other laws and governments are regarded as growing out of the depravity of man, and in rebellion to God. Nevertheless, they receive the protection of the government of the land. And often appeal to it in their dealings with the world.

This government is different from any other government in the world; yet, in some of its features, it is like Catholicism and Mormonism. Its miracles, visions, revelations, superstitions, and confession of sins, by which the elders obtain unlimited sway over the minds of their subjects.

The seat of government is called by them 'the head of influence.' Every law, permanent order, and important transaction must have the sanction of the ministry here. The ministry here is composed of four persons, two males and two females. The first in the ministry is simply styled elder, and appoints the other three. And has power to depose them at any time and to appoint others. The other male member is designated only by the appellation of 'brother,' joined to his christian name. He acts in subordination to the first, and as a sort of Prime minister to him. One of the females is also the superior of the other and has a subordinate authority in the female department. She is styled eldress, the other is designated as 'sister.' These titles are always joined to their christian names when addressing them or speaking of them. These people are very strict in the formality of calling every body whom they address, or speak of, by their christian name, and in never giving them any title of distinction.

The head minister who resides at New Lebanon, appoints his successor, and the ministry, or bishops, in the societies throughout the denomination. So that his authority is supreme. Though, doubtless, in matters of importance, he counsels with his subordinates in office. The offices in the denomination are graduated as follows:—1st. The ministry at New Lebanon, whose authority is supreme. 2nd. A subordinate ministry, appointed by the ministry at New Lebanon (or 'the head of influence') over the different portions of the communion. 3rd. Every family has its elders and deacons.

The elders and deacons have authority in the family over which they are appointed, limited only by their superiors in office. They are appointed by the ministry of the diocese in which they belong. The ministry have authority over their diocese, and every member of it, limited only by 'the head of influence.' Every family elder is a petty despot, and a very implicit and servile obedience to him is required of all the members of the family. Every elder in the ministry is a bigger despot, as all the family elders, even, must humble themselves in perfect obedience to him. The elder at the 'head of influence' is a perfect pope in authority. He is the successor of Mother Anne, and is vested with her authority, or the authority of Christ in his second appearing.

The deaconship of each family is composed of four persons. Two males and two females. As a general thing one deacon has the superintendance of agriculture and animals; the other of finance and exchange. The deaconesses have the superintendance of domestic economy, manufactures, &c. But these are subordinate to the elders, and must give account to them of all their doings. The eldership of each family also is composed of four persons, commonly designated as first and second elder, and first and second eldress. Although, according to the rules of Shakerism, only one is elder, one eldress. The other two brother and sister, who stand with them. The last are subordinate to the first. The ministry are also constituted in the same way. Elder and eldress with their companions, or the brother and sister who stand with them. Some of these bishops have the charge of two or more societies,—others of only one.

It is expected of all these officers that they will be engaged in some useful employment, except when engaged in the discharge of their official duties. The ministry, however, do not labor with, nor associate familiarly with the common members. They have their shops by themselves, and live and labor by themselves. They live in the upper part of the meeting-house, and have their shops contiguous. Two shops, one for the females and one for the males. The common members are not permitted to call on the ministry for any purpose whatever, unless, indeed, the ministry should need them and send for them. The elders may call on them at their shops if they have important business with them, or important communications to make to them; but may not call at their dwelling. The ministry often have business with the elders, and send for them to come to their *shop.* Their dwelling is peculiarly holy. Nevertheless, the ministry often visit the several families; but in this case they retire immediately with the elders to their rooms, and there remain until the family is formally called together, when they formally present themselves and address them in a very formal, though affectionate manner. This exclusiveness on their part is necessary to the maintenance of their authority and dignity. They sometimesd eign to speak to individuals, but seldom. Although the ministry live by themselves in the meeting-house, they are boarded and cared for by the church family. They generally come to this house to their meals, but do not eat in the same room with the family. And when they take a meal at the house of any other family, there is a room called the ministry's dining room, where they eat by themselves, and where the very best is provided. Indeed great reverence is paid to the ministry.

But how is their authority maintained, and how are their laws enforced? How is this despotism maintained in the midst of a republic, where every one can appeal to the laws of the land for protection against their tyranny, and can withdraw from this people at his pleasure?

In answering this question, it will be necessary to expose their general policy, which involves their pretensions to revelations. Their whirling, twisting, bowing, twitching, jerking, leaping, falling, trancing, and contortions;—unknown tongues, shouting, singing, &c.;—confession of sins, form of dress, language, and many other formalities. Their peculiar doctrines, united interests, &c. For all these are made to bear upon one point, all are directed to the attainment of one end, viz: the complete subjection of the common members to the elders and ministry.

"Simplicity and obedience," is the stereotyped text of all preaching and exhortation among this people. Obey and follow your lead. Keep your union with the elders, and you will do well enough. Obedience to them is obedience to God. " Hands to work and hearts to God," is also a very important motto, handed down from Mother Anne. Industry, economy, and neatness, have the promise of great rewards in the world to come. But all is nothing without simple, chlidlike, and unreserved obedience to the elders. The obedient cannot fail of heaven. The disobedient cannot be saved. This is the only, " the little straight and narrow way."

The government is professedly a divine government. All appointments to office, all laws and orders profess to come from God. They are not of man, but of God.

Formerly the laws and orders for the government of societies and families, came directly from the ministry without any pretensions to special revelation. Yet, as they were supposed to be anointed by the Holy Spirit of God, which guided them in all their *official* duties, at least, their authority was divine, their requirements inspired, and of course, divine. But lest they should seem to some to lack the divine sanction and authority, they have, in later years, been renewed by special inspiration, through the principal prophet, who, of course, resides at New Lebanon, the head of influence.

As they were revealed, they were written out in two books. The first of these books is termed the " Holy Laws." The other, " the Order Book." These books contain nearly all the permanent laws and regulations which prevail in the denomination. Every family has a written copy of them ; and they are read to the members of the family by the elders, once or twice in every year. A violation of any of these laws or orders is declared to be a sin to be repented of and confessed.

Why these revealed laws and orders should be written in two volumes, instead of one, and distinguished by " Holy laws," and " Order book," I am not able to tell. They seem all to be of the same general character, all equally inspired, and the violation of any of them equally sinful. The terms *law* and *order*, as used in their government, are synonymous. Besides these there are some few orders pre-go before the world. Such, for example, as the laws relating to the education of children, the reading of books and papers by the members; the contemptuous manner in which the arts and sciences are spoken of, &c. The elder had by some means, become satisfied that it was my intention to withdraw from them, though I had not declared that intention, nor made any preparations for withdrawing. Rather than I should hear these very objectionable portions and run the risk of my exposing them to the world, he would not read them at all until another year should come round. Hoping, no doubt, that I had forgotten them, as I had never heard them but once. But I had remembered and already written down some of them, and shall bring them in, in their proper place and order.

The book containing these laws states, that these laws were written by God himself, at the intercession, prayers, and supplications of the two anointed ones, Christ and Mother Ann, to be established on earth. My memory will not enable me to give these laws in the language of the book, or in the order of the chapters; or even to give an idea of more than a few of them.

The laws themselves require that the book containing them should be kept by the elders and not used in common. They require to be read once a year for six years. I asked the privilege of reading these laws, but was refused on the ground that they were not circulated in the family. There is another book called the "Order Book" which I also asked the privilege of seeing but was refused on the same ground. The orders themselves forbid it. This book is similar to the Holy laws; it came after it, and seems to be a sort of supplement to it, entering into more minute particulars of the government. There is also another small book which relates to eating and drinking. Prohibits the use of all intoxicating drinks, the use of tobacco in all its forms, limits the use of pork to once a day; and enjoins strict temperance and frugality in eating and drinking, I also asked the privilege of seeing this book, but was refused, as there was a law in the same that none should see it but the elders and ministry.

This enabled the elders to reject my several requests to see these books with a better grace, but I think the true reason of their refusal was a suspicion, or fear, that I should expose their contents to the world. For when they are read in connexion, they are so absurd and ridiculous, that it seems impossible that any intelligent thinking person should ever believe in their inspiration. Yet the common members generally do not indulge a doubt but they are all they profess to be. These revelations themselves place the ministry and elders above the laws, if not above God. In every revelation of this kind, it is provided that, " if the beloved ministry and elders in their wisdom, the holy wisdom with which I have anointed them," think best to establish it among my people, saith the Lord, it becomes a law, subject however to be by them repeated or set aside according to their judgment. In these books the following expressions are frequently used. I may not get them verbatim, (but as near as I could remember until I had written them down.) The Lord in proclaiming his laws to the people of his Zion on earth in his own name, says, This shall be so and so, if your beloved Lead have union to it. " If it is thought best by my holy anointed on earth." " If the beloved ministry and elders give it their union," &c. (The beloved Lead, the Holy anointed are the ministry and elders, and their union to a thing is their approval of it.) People who are entirely unacquainted with the Shakers may think it incredible, that they should attempt to palm off such absurdities as revelation. That the Lord should make his own wisdom subordinate to human wisdom. And submit his ordinances to the ministry and elders to receive their sanction and approbation before they can be established. As much as to say, God has been induced by the intercessions, prayers and supplications of Christ, and Mother Ann, to write out and reveal the Holy laws and sundry other laws for the government of his people the Shakers. But he don't know certainly as it is best that they should be established. Therefore he submits them to you beloved Lead, the elders and ministry ; they being wiser than God will *certainly* know whether it is best to establish them or not. These are facts well known to all who have been members of the Shaker community within a few years past. And it is a fair specimen of their general management. Not long previous to the time for reading the Holy laws, viz., the birth day of Mother Ann, I talked with the elders about these laws, and asked the privilege of perusing them, but was refused. I inquired when they would probably be read again. I also asked the elder if he should read them all; as I observed when he read them before, he turned over some leaves without reading. Barnabas (the second elder) in answer to this observed, that some leaves were left blank for the ministry to fill up. So the laws of God are nothing until they are *perfected* and sanctioned by "the Holy ministry," as they are called. And it is expressly provided near the close of the book containing them, that if they have the approbation of the blessed ministry, they may affix to them their names and seals. And doubtless the original copy of these laws were signed and sealed by them. As though God could not perfect his own work, but left blank leaves to be filled up by any human being! or, as though the names and seals of men could add any thing to them. What reflecting mind can receive such pretensions for divine truth! They are more palpably absurd than any thing to be found in Mormonism or any other fanaticism in the world.

The members are very frequently exhorted to "keep every little order given for our protection." All the tyranny and oppression perpetrated upon the members, is done under the name of "*protection*." And it is said to them, "you will yet see the day that you will be thankful for this severity; you will know that it is your protection. And the great desideratum in a Shaker's life is obedience to the elders and ministry. *A simple and willing obedience.* This is every thing. It is indeed the foundation of peace and harmony among them. It is their "*protection*." There must be authority on the one part and implicit obedience on the other. Or, in other words, it is tyranny and slavery.

The holy laws require of the church order that they shall be more strict in their conduct, more circumspect in all their goings forth; that they may be an example unto other orders. For says God in these laws, " Ye are nearer to God ; and are called to be more pure and holy." And the other orders are commanded to reverence this order as being nearer to God, more holy, &c. They are forbidden to hire men from the world to work for them, if it can possibly be dispensed with. And when it is necessary to hire, it is required that the " world's men" work by themselves, with one to oversee them, who is appointed in order. That is, by the authority of the elders. For it is said, " believers" have come under great loss in this way. " Their young men have been corrupted by working with the children of the unclean, and have turned away, who otherwise might have been here now." We are exhorted to do our work ourselves, and not hire wicked worldlings. " But the elders and ministry must be the judges in these matters, saith the Lord." It is required that all commerce, and all intercourse for any purpose whatever with the world should " cease" as much as possible. For it is said, we cannot have intercourse with them and not be defiled. We must not therefore trade with them, nor visit, nor correspond, nor associate with them any more than is absolutely necessary. They are denominated " the wicked of this world," " the children of the unclean," " those who have not confessed their sins, &c." And we must have nothing to do with them unless they come to confess their sins. Then it is required that they shall have a privilege to confess their sins, and set out in the way and work of God. And no distinction is to be made, no partiality shown to any on account of wealth, or learning, or other consideration. But all are to be treated upon a ground of equality. In taking in children, it is strictly forbidden to be influenced at all by the prospect of property with the children, immediately, or remotely." " But we should rather receive the children of the poor."

After having listened to the reading of the fourteen parts which were revealed through father James ; and be-

fore listening to the other six parts revealed by the Holy angel, we were required all to rise and make eight low bows in concert. And then four more low bows, in concert, all repeating aloud at the same time, these words: " I will obey thy Holy laws, O Zion."
And then commenced the reading of the other six parts. Where at the commencement, the following occurs. " It was by the prayers, supplications, and intercessions of Christ and Mother, father James, and father William, and all your heavenly parents, that God granted leave to the Holy, and proclaiming angel to read the other six parts ; beginning where father James left off, viz., at the 15th part, and reading to the 20th, inclusive. At the close of the reading of these other six parts, we were required again (by the book) to rise as before, and make three low bows, at the same time repeating in concert these words : " Love, love, love from God our heavenly Father."

"Laws in relation to cutting the Hair and trimming the Beard."

" The hair shall not be left unnecessarily long before, nor behind. It shall be cut square across the forehead, and thence in a line with the bottom of the ear. Those who have a thick growth of hair, shall have it cut as often as once in four or five weeks. The brethren shall shave twice a week, viz., Wednesdays and Saturdays, and at no other time, unless one is going a journey, or for some such cause. The ear locks," (probably whiskers are here meant) " shall be cut square with the bottom of the ear."
It is forbidden to use intoxicating drinks except as a medicine. " But if any who have passed the meridian of life feel that they must have a little cider, the quantity shall be regulated by the ministry. If any feel it to be necessary they may use a very little small beer in the summer season." At this period there was a short intermission ; and when the reading recommenced, the elder evidently passed over a considerable portion. Some of which related (as I remember from the reading a year previous) to the manner in which the sisters should fillet their hair.

The fashion, color, and quantity of clothing both for the brethren and sisters. All of which are very minutely described, even by the finger of God. The sisters are required to comb their hair clean, and straight back from the forepart of the head, and fasten it in a knot upon the back part with a pin made for that purpose. And to wear a straight plain muslin cap, which shall come so closely over the face as to conceal the hair entirely. The remainder of the dress of the brethren and sisters, is nearly the same as was in the height of the world's fashion sixty-five, or seventy years ago. Except the fashion of the brethren's frocks, which I believe is entirely new and original.

The custom among them in regard to the use of intoxicating drinks, notwithstanding the prohibitory laws. In this society at Hancock, or the " city of peace," the elder of the church family, William Demming, and natural brother of the late minister of this society, being by nature well endowed with alimentiveness and mirthfulness, loves a joke, a witty remark, and a glass of wine. He keeps his brandy and other stimulants without reserve or concealment. The ministry are abundantly provided by the sisters of the church with wines, cordials, &c. The elder of the family with which we were connected, is in the regular daily use of cider-brandy ; but very privately. After the family moved into the new house, the old one was used for the sisters workshops, sick rooms for the brethren and sisters ; farmer's sitting-room, &c. In one of the entries, or passages into this building, was a little side-cup-board, in which the elder found his glass of cider-brandy placed there regularly every day, and as regularly by him emptied of its contents. It was placed there by sister Nancy, the 2d eldress, and also the family nurse, who had the care of the medicines, including the cider-brandy and other spirits. This society have considerable orcharding, and make a very large quantity of cider, for these temperance days. They also have a small distillery in which a part of the cider is distilled to brandy. Hence their supply of this article. The 2d elder, brother Barnabas Sprague, being feeble in health, also feels the need of the frequent use of spiritous liquors in the form of bitters, cordials, &c. There are also a few private members in this family past the meridian of life, to whom the elders deal out a quart of cider a day, regularly, in accordance with the order of the ministry, except on Saturdays in the afternoon and Sundays; when they are required to abstain entirely. With these exceptions, the common members practice total abstinence; many of the aged voluntarily.

These examples, I have no doubt, afford a fair sample of the practice of the denomination on this subject. The fact relative to Shaker temperance is this. The temperance cause had gained a mighty influence over the world around, and this people were becoming a reproach for continuing in an unpopular and immoral practice. It became necessary that something should be done. Therefore they had a special revelation covering the whole ground. And a very accommodating one it is. In the book concerning eating and drinking, a book distinct from the Holy laws; this subject is treated minutely. After prohibiting the use of intoxicating drinks, and tobacco, and pronouncing a terrible curse upon all who should afterwards use any; the Lord, very absurdly it seems to me, directs that all above a certain age may use a little spirit if they feel as though they could not do without it; also a little cider. And all above forty years of age may use tobacco temperately. And then in this connexion the Lord exhorts them all to volunteer in the practice of total abstinence, promising a reward to all who would do so. Accordingly many of the aged voluntarily took up their cross in this matter and abstain from all these things.

As to any inconsistency on the part of the ministry and elders, in making use of these forbidden fruits, the case is thus. *They are above the laws.* Having power by special provision, to repeal, or set them aside in part, or as a whole, or to make such additions to them as they in their wisdom shall think proper. Consequently it is no sin for them to use these things notwithstanding the prohibitions of God. But I will return again for a short season to the Holy laws.

After the chapter, or portion, in relation to the clothing, head dressing, &c., came a portion on eating. Here the elder passed over so much, and so irregularly, that I could not keep the run of it. He commenced in the middle of a subject, reading, " we must use these things as sparingly as possible. It is recommended those who have been in the habit of using a large portion, should not use more than half as much." The elder here explained that this had reference to eating fat meat, &c.

There was also a portion on the subject of " gifts," or inspirations of the Holy Spirit. It was required that no times, or seasons, should set for the fulfilment of any predictions; and it is said " that the setting of times and seasons is an evidence that the gift is not of God." And God requires that, " when any of my children are under operations, that those standing round should not be conversing together, but should give respectful attention to the operations of the Spirit." It is required also, that if any brother, or sister, feels that they have a gift of inspiration, they must go to the elders and ask leave to manifest it. Every thing of this kind must come in *order*, and must have the " union of the elders." It is clear that if times and seasons are set, predictions might be falsified, not being fulfilled at the time specified. Which would tend to overthrow Shaker revelation. Hence the prohibition of setting " times and seasons." And if these things did not come in order, that is, through the elders, that the true predictions may be selected and the false thrown away, through the multiplicity of them coming from so many prophets and prophetesses, there would be so much conflict and jargon that no person living could profit by it. As Br. Barnabas the 2d elder said to me one evening while conversing upon this subject, " the elders have a hard time of it in this hurrycane of gifts, to know what is revelation and what is not." The person under inspiration may, or may not, be mistaken; but the elders are the judges in all these matters.

At the close of this book (the Holy laws,) it is provided that if the beloved ministry approve of what is contained in it, there is nothing which prohibits their putting names and seals to the same."

The regulations contained in the "order book," profess also to have come by inspiration, or renewed by special inspiration; as many of these, and also of the "Holy laws" were originally made and given out by the ministry. They are considered as equally sacred and equally binding with the Holy laws. Some of them, however, seem to be a mere repetition of the Holy laws, as nearly as I can remember. Never having heard this book read but once, I do not remember them very distinctly from the reading; but from hearing them repeated verbally, and from being called to observe them, I can give the substance of many of them. In doing this, however, I may mistake sometimes the "Holy laws" for the orders, and, the "orders" for the "Holy laws."

The orders forbid the reading of any newspaper after supper, on Saturday, or any book except the Bible, and books printed by "Believers." The same is forbidden on the Sabbath, and Sabbath evening. The common members are not generally allowed to read newspapers at all, at any time. The elders and deacons, or, the "lead," as they are called, indulge themselves in this way, and in some families the privilege is sometimes extended further. It is considered very dangerous for the common members to read books and papers printed by the world.

A signal is given half an hour before meal time; another ten minutes before, when the brethren assemble in what is called at the east house, the farmers sitting room. The sisters gather in the Hall, or some convenient place. At the expiration of ten minutes, another signal is given, when all repair to the tables in regular order. The brethren in at one door of the dining-room, and the sisters at another. They move in single file; first on the lead, the elder, second elder, first and second deacon, then the next best, and so on, the boys in the rear with their overseer, to keep them right. The sisters also in the same order. Thus they place themselves around the table, and never changing places at the table, every one knows his place.

When every one stands before his plate with hands folded according to Divine law, he looks at the elder; and as the elder begins to kneel, all simultaneously follow his example. It is required that they spread their pocket-handkerchiefs before them on their seats as they kneel; close their eyes, fold their hands, remaining a few moments in this attitude of devotion. They rise with the elder, sit down and take their food in silence. Rise from the table with the elder, perform again their silent devotions and retire in the same order as they came in. All conversation in the dining room, or hall is strictly forbidden. The law says, there shall be no smiling, or winking at each other at the table, but my people should take their meals in the fear of the Lord. The brethren and sisters do not sit at the same table when they eat, though in the same room. The sisters who prepare the food also wait on the tables. When an individual wishes anything which is not before him, he beckons to him a sister, who is in waiting, and makes known to her his wish in a low whisper. It is strictly forbidden that hired men, or any world's people, (those who have not confessed their sins,) should eat in the same room, and at the same time with believers. There is therefore a room called the world's dining-room, where visitors from the world, and others are served.

These people take their food hastily. Probably the time of eating, including their devotions before and after, does not vary much from fifteen minutes. It is very common for them to eat a portion of their meal directly from the platter, without first taking the food on to their plates. This custom as one devout sister observed, is in union. That is, the elders practice it. Of course nothing could be said against it. The tables are so arranged that four persons help themselves from the same platter. One tumbler, or small mug, also, answers for four persons, to drink water from, which is replenished from a large pitcher. It is common for them to drink with food in their mouth, and without wiping their lips. This custom to people of refinement would be disgusting; as some particles of grease might often be detected upon this pure and otherwise delightful beverage, which would very much impair its relish. And one would be thought very fastidious who should request a tumbler for himself alone. So also with their rice puddings, oyster soups, succotash, &c., each is furnished with a common table-spoon which he plies from platter to mouth.

It is required of the brethren and sisters that they kneel in devotion to God, every night when they retire to bed, and when they rise up in the morning. It is required that they lay straight in bed and take their rest in the fear of God. When they go into "laboring meetings" as it is called, that is, meeting for their usual religious exercises, they are required to arrange themselves in a particular order, the brethren upon one side, and the sisters upon the other, facing each other. Each to lock his hands before him, with right thumb over the left. And in kneeling, every one must bend the right knee first. In union meeting, all are required to fold their hands in the same manner, and to set both feet square on the floor. It is forbidden to sit crosslegged, or in any unbecoming manner. It is forbidden to write any thing without the knowledge and approval of the elders. Every letter sent, or received, must be read to the elders. And no one must keep any secret from the elders. It is forbidden that a brother and sister converse together, or *be* together without a third person. The brethren are forbidden to go into the sisters rooms without rapping and being bid come in. And the sisters are under the same restraint in going to the brethren's rooms. But says the word of God, "The elders are not bound by this law." The brethren are required to remain in the dwelling-house on the Sabbath, except while doing the necessary chores. They are not permitted to walk out or indulge in any amusement whatever; or to read any books, or newspapers, except the Bible, and books printed by believers. There is usually one meeting of the several families at the meeting-house, and each family has one meeting for worship in its own dwelling. The brethren are forbidden to be at any of the shops over five minutes at a time on the Sabbath. But during the other days of the week they are forbidden to be in the dwelling-house except to take their meals, or for some necessary business. They may come in in the evening to attend the usual meeting.

Thus is every position and movement, all the conduct and intercourse of the members marked out with this precision and particularity, by specific laws and orders written by the finger of the Almighty, and given at the prayers and intercessions of Christ and Mother Ann. And it is declared by the same authority, that every violation of these laws, or any of them, is sin. And must be confessed to the elders before going into meeting. And it is believed that when any sin is confessed thus, it is forgiven and blotted out from God's record. And the sinner stands fully justified. This is Shaker justification.

Implicit obedience, not only to all laws, and orders, which come in this way, but to every wish expressed, and every direction of the elders and ministry, is constantly held up as the greatest virtue and excellence to which any can attain; and is generally believed to be such by the members. They often speak of going " forth in obedience." That is, they march, dance, shake, whirl round, jump, leap, fall down, have gifts, visions, revelations, speak in unknown tongues, or talk gibberish; all in obedience to the elders. Obedience to the elders is the same as obedience to God. So also, in all manner of labor among them, they follow their lead; every thing is directed by the elders and deacons. Who, also, are required to labor with the rest. The common members are not allowed to have any particular interest in the property, or labor. Their work is laid out, and they go on and perform it according to direction, like so many slaves, or as the horses and oxen. Indeed they are most thoroughly enslaved. Every waking hour has its duties, and the sleeping hours are limited. The hours of the day are devoted to labor, and the evening to religious exercises, or what are called " union" meetings. At the close of which, every one is required to retire to his sleeping-room, kneel, go to bed, lay straight and take his rest in the fear of God. All rise early at the tinkling of the bell, a regular and certain warning. The labors of the day, and the same routine of duties is gone through with, day after day, from the time one commences his Shaker life until he enters his grave. The grand motto of all is, "Hands to work, and hearts to God." This motto was given by Mother Ann, in the first of the faith, and its observance has ever been regarded as necessary to their success. It is constantly held up as an encouragement to labor, that their rewards in the life to come, will be somewhat in proportion to their industry here. Thus it is with the Shaker life; he has no moments he can call his own; every hour has its appointed duties, and he must toil on through this monotonous life. Toiling with his hands through the day, dancing, and shaking through the evening, and, if there are any moments for thought, his thoughts must be confined to this "straight and narrow way." All worldly knowledge is as much as possible precluded. The arts, and sciences "as ye call them," (this is an expression of contempt used in the Holy laws,) are considered as entirely unworthy the notice of a Shaker. And he has no hope of any thing different in the world to come. For all the visionists represent the spirits of the departed as subject to the same strict discipline, and the same government as those who remain. The same uniform dress, language, religious exercises, obedience to their lead, &c. If this is not enslaving both soul and body, then are the Shakers free, and all our ideas of slavery are erroneous.

But it is very natural to inquire, how is this thing accomplished? how is it possible that naturally intelligent people should thus be enslaved in this land of light and freedom? In answering this question, I shall be led to speak farther of the policy of their government in regard to education, and of their superstition.

Education.

The laws and orders strictly prohibit the study of Chemistry, Philosophy, Astronomy, Phrenology, Physiology. In reading the laws on this subject, the elder read a long list of ologies, concluding with, "&c." Which I conclude was meant by the author to include all the sciences whose name ends in *Ology*. As Geology, Theology, Zoology, &c. These I think were named in the list, or catalogue of sciences prohibited. Nevertheless the Shakers have schools for the children taken in among them. And the laws specify what may be taught in them, viz., "Reading, writing, a little arithmetic, a little grammar, and a little geography." This is the expression, as nearly as I can recollect. It is evidently their policy to limit their education as much as possible, and seem to conform to the law of the state. The schools in the society where we resided were not under the superintendence of the town School Committee. All the sciences are prohibited, except such as the laws of the land compel them to teach. God says (according to Shaker revelation) a "little" or "small portion" of these may be taught in the schools.

The children are allowed three months schooling in a year. The girls have their schooling in the summer, and the boys in the winter. Girls and boys do not attend the same school. The girls were allowed to attend school until they were fifteen years of age, and the boys until they were sixteen. This completed their education. Their teachers were of themselves, and as a general thing, their qualifications would not entitle them to an approval of the town's committee. And being limited by the "Holy laws" to the teaching "a small portion" of the lower branches, it can easily be judged what the state of education among them would be. Observation shows it to be in accordance with their advantages. There are very few among them, who receive their education, who can construct their own language according to the rules of grammar. I had an opportunity to read and hear read compositions from those who were thought the most competent to write in the society. They were generally very incorrect. Joseph Wicker, their chief prophet, is undoubtedly the best educated of any one who was educated in this society. He has doubtless gone very much beyond what is allowed by the Holy laws. There are other instances where individuals have broken the orders of the denomination and improved their minds beyond what is allowed. One young man (Solomon Wollison,) with whom I was intimate there, by secreting books and stealing opportunities to read them, has outgrown his slavery, and is regarded by them as a ruined man. With a few such exceptions, "*book larnin*" as they call it, is very scarce. And "the arts, and sciences, as ye call them," are despised by them. It is the policy of the "Lead" to keep worldly knowledge as far off as possible; it interferes with their authority and makes them trouble. The elders assured me that those who got much learning did not do well. They were apt to become disobedient and "turn off." In conversing with the elders on the subject of education, I told them very plainly that their children did not have so good advantages as our common schools in the world afforded; and that their young men were not qualified to do common business in the world. The elder in reply, very justly and pertinently remarked, "that they did not educate their children for the world, but to remain there." It is clearly the belief of the "lead" that the less their people know of every thing, except that routine of duties which make up the life of a Shaker, the better "believers" they make, Or, in plain words, it is their policy, and for the welfare of the sect, to keep them as ignorant as possible. I will here transcribe a short dialogue which I had with a young man from the Shaker society in Tyringham. I place it here only because it is a good expression in their own language, of their sentiments on education. Great pains are taken to impress the idea upon the mind of every youth. This young man had a privilege to come over to our society with Leonard Allen, who came on some business. The young man came into the shop where I wrought, and introduced himself as Richard Vandoozenbury, said he was fifteen years old. He seemed as intelligent and sprightly as any young man of his age I had seen among the Shakers. Among other conversation I asked him about the school in their society, and observed that his time for schooling had nearly expired, he being nearly sixteen years old. This was Jan. 1845.

He says, "Yea, I don't go now. I have been in the shop about a month, I thought I'd druther work in the shop than do nothing. I could'nt larn nothin in school. The brother that keeps the school had'nt got much larnin; he broke his leg very bad last winter, and could'nt do nothin else, and so they let him keep school. He teaches the little boys to read."

I asked does he teach grammar?

"Nay, he ha'nt got much larnin."

Did you ever study grammar?

"Yea, I studied grammar a little last winter."

Did you get so as to parse?

"Nay. I don't care to have much grammar. I don't want much larnin.

I find it is a bad thing to know too much. Better not know quite enough than to know too much. If I can know enough to obey my lead, and do as they want to have me, it it enough for me."

Have you studied arithmetic?

"Yea, some."

What arithmetic did you study?

"I don't know."

Adam's?

"Nay."

Smith's?

"Nay."

Emerson's?

"Nay. It was one that had twelve members. Twelve is the highest degree. I never went further than eight."

What rule was that?

"I don't remember."

Was it practice? or, fractions?

"I guess it was fractions."

Now, this young man was a good "believer." Such an one as would maintain a good union with his beloved Lead; at least, so long as he maintained these opinions. He was imbued with the right spirit for a good Shaker. A spirit of obedience to his lead. This is the one thing needful. He was fairly prejudiced against knowledge, and this was his safety. Knowledge is the bane of Shakerism. It renders their young people restless and disobedient, and carries them away to the wicked world. Therefore it is the policy of the Lead to keep them as ignorant as possible. This is necessary to their existence as a people. They cannot live in the light; their doctrines, or practices, will not bear investigation. Their superstition, and slavery seek to hide themselves in the utmost darkness. But God is a God of light, and truth ever seeks and demands investigation. Truth, liberty, and light are most nearly related. And so are error, darkness of mind and slavery. In order to be a good Shaker, the intellect must be crushed; as well as all else that is natural to man. This is one of the means by which their government is maintained.

Inspiration; or communion with the Spiritual World.

This is the most important, and to many will be the most interesting part of Shakerism. Here the sublime and the ridiculous are brought into close juxtapositon, and mirthfulness is strongly moved upon. Yet all is admirably calculated to bring the simple ones under the power and influence of their Lead. They carry the matter of inspiration to a very great extent. All the laws of their government were (as I have before stated) written out by the finger of God, and were delivered to a Holy angel, in answer to the prayers and supplications of Christ, and Mother Ann, to be read to mortal man for the observance of his people, or his Zion on earth. In almost every meeting for worship, some of their prophets have a communication from the spiritual world. They have regular prophets in every family, who are set apart, or anointed by the ministry. I think there are four persons in each family, set apart for this purpose. Two brothers, and two sisters. I did not have the pleasure of witnessing the ceremony of anointing. But received an account of it from one who had been anointed. Which I will give in his own language.

"The ceremony was not very imposing, those who received this gift were called before the ministry, pronounced worthy, and received on their knees, by imposition of hands, and other appropriate motions, the crowning, and clothing, appropriate to the official capacity in which they were to act. They were informed that it was for them to have these gifts, (of seeing, hearing, prophesying, &c., in spiritual matters,) and, that they must go forth in them, in perfect obedience to, and union with their visible lead, this to be the test as to the quality of their gifts."

The crowning, and clothing here spoken of, must not be taken literally. For the crown, and the dress, could be seen only by those whose eyes were opened to spiritual things. They were a gift from the Spiritual world. They were to have these gifts : it is promised through the beloved ministry. If they do not have them it will be their own fault. They must labor for them; that is, whirl round with their eyes closed, bow, and writhe the body, and direct the mind with excessive energy to the attainment of these gifts. And knowing that the elders, and beloved ministry will be disappointed if they do not obtain the gifts, it is not strange that many of them work themselves up into the belief that they are inspired; talk gibberish for an unknown tongue; see spirits, and many wonderful things. It is not strange that some shrewd ones who have small conscientiousness, should play their part of the game in guile. It is not strange even that some should magnetize themselves, or throw themselves into a trance, and honestly relate wonderful things.

But all these gifts of visions, and revelation, must be in obedience to, and union with their visible lead. That is, they must go forth in these gifts, whenever the elders intimate to them to do so. And they must have such gifts, and revelations as the elders can approve and sanction. If the elders approve and sanction the gift, it is a real gift, a true revelation. If it is not in accordance with the faith, and the mind of the elders, it is a delusion, and is false. For this is to be the test of the genuineness of the gift. It must be obtained by them, in obedience to, and union with their visible Lead.

It should be observed, the fact that some are anointed to be prophets, does not preclude others from having gifts. The elders encourage others to labor for them. And many do labor for them successfully. I will here introduce some specimens of these gifts—and predictions.

Family Meetings; A sober Meeting, the first I attended.

The first Shaker meeting I attended was when I visited them before taking my family there. This might very justly be called a sober meeting. For there was no dancing, or shaking, no gift of visions, or prophesying. But a grave exhortation from the elder, a few songs, and the marching of the audience. In marching, they made the circuit of the Hall, keeping time with the music; the singers standing in the center.

This was but a family meeting, in the Hall of their dwelling. Every dwelling-house, is provided with a Hall, for the assembled family to worship in. This Hall in the house where we resided is about forty feet by twenty feet. The floor is perfectly level, and well polished. The room is neatly finished, and well lighted. The Hall is entered by two doors from the common entry, or passage way; one for the brethren, and the other for the sisters. A half an hour previous to the commencement of the meeting for worship, a bell is rung to notify the family that it is "*retire time.*" That is, according to divine order, the members of the family are all required to retire to their several apartments, and spend the half hour in silent meditation. It is against order to speak, or laugh, during "retire time." And if any one so far forgets himself through fatigue, or indolence, as to fall asleep during retire time, he, or she, is required by divine order, (and indeed all orders and laws are divine, because all come by special revelations to arise immediately on awaking and make three low bows. Whether this law is strictly observed in all cases is a matter of doubt. The brother with whom I roomed was a very devout and indeed a very intelligent Shaker, and I presume never caught himself a napping during retire time. If he had, I have no doubt he would have instantly arose on waking, and inflicted upon himself the penalty of the law. And I should have witnessed his grey and venerable head, making three low bows in profound silence and solemnity. Probably some who are less devout occasionally fall alseep, (as they are often weary, the meeting being after the labors of the day are closed,) but do not inflict upon themselves the penalty of the law. At the close of the half hour the bell is again rung, the brethren, and sisters emerge from their apartments, and preceded by the Eldress, march into the Hall; the sisters entering one door, and the brethren the other; and range themselves in rank and file order. The elders standing at the head of the first, or front rank, and Deacons next, and the principal singers next; the younger members standing in the rear. These two phalanxes, one of sisters, the other of brethren, formed across the Hall, face each other. The space between these two bodies is called the altar. Or, there is an imaginary, or spiritual altar in this space, near where the elders stand. This space between the bodies is about five feet wide at the head, or between the elders gradually widening to the foot of the ranks, where it is ten or twelve feet wide. They are very particular to stand in this form.

Having placed themselves in this form, all standing erect, with folded hands, the right thumb over the left according to divine order, the exercises commence, usually with a song, or short hymn. Followed by an exhortation from the elder, then another song; then the exercises of marching, dancing, &c. Their music is vocal. Instrumental music is strictly prohibited.

Having arrived at the "City of Peace" with my family, we attended the family meeting in the evening. We did not take part in the exercises, but were seated as visitors, wife at one end of the Hall, and self at the other. After the usual singing and exhortation, the elder says, "The brethren and sisters may go forth in a quick lively manner." The singers immediately took their position, which in this dance, was in a single line, with their backs to the wall, at about an equal distance from either end of the Hall. The rest of the family arranged themselves, so that the brethren occupied one end of the Hall, and the sisters the other; without any other order than, they stood facing the place occupied by the singers, and the hands folded before them with the right thumb over the left. The brethren having laid off their coats, and the sisters laid aside their handkerchiefs were ready to "labor." The singers struck up a lively tune, (instrumental music is not allowed) when all start off in a lively trot, making a small circuit in an irregular manner, the brethren and sisters not mingling together, but each occupying either end of the Hall; when they came to the set of the tune, they faced towards the singers, and shuffled in time. When this had continued for a short time, the singing ceased and the dancing for a few moments while the singers could take breath; when it recommenced. This is the usual course in these exercises. Directly after the exercise of dancing commenced, one of the sisters commenced turning round very rapidly, and directly another followed her example, and then another, and another, until five or six were engaged in this operation. The rest of the audience continued their exercises of dancing, singing, marching, &c. This turning is not upon the toe, or heel, but by a continual stepping of one foot around the other, generally with the eyes closed. They turn from ten minutes to three quarters of an hour, and sometimes much longer. I have seen the young sisters turn three quarters of an hour without any intermission, or appearance of dizziness, at the rate of from forty to sixty turns in a minute. This they pretend is done by inspiraration; and is held up as an evidence of inspiration. And indeed it was the strongest evidence of their inspiration which I saw while among them. When I first witnessed this rapid turning so long continued, it seemed impossible that it could be done by natural powers. But some of the young brethren who had been in the practice of turning, but who were not ambitious of being thought inspired, assured me there was no inspiration in the matter, all the skill being acquired by practice. And I observed that the young sisters were trained to this exercise very early. I frequently noticed with admiration a company of young girls belonging to the " Second family," at the meeting-house, on the Sabbath, who were too young to join with the rest of the audience, laboring by themselves in one corner of the house ; occasionally turning very rapidly, and skilfully, for a considerable length of time. I observed also, that new beginners in this art, were very unskilful ; turning only a short time, moderately, often staggering, and sometimes falling down. Although my marvellousness is large, and I had a desire that the pretentions of the Shakers should prove true ; yet when I came to examine the matter, I became thoroughly convinced that there was no supernatural assistance in this exercise in any case. At this first meeting attended by myself and wife, there was evidently an extra effort made to produce an impression. The anointed ones labored for their gifts with much zeal, when the singing and dancing ceased as it did at intervals, and these intervals were protracted as the excitement increased, there was a death-like stillness, as though every mind felt that there was a Divine presence. No sound was heard except a slight rustling of the clothes of the turners, as they whirled swiftly round, and made a gentle tapping with their feet on the floor as they stepped around. An enthusiast who might be present would be inclined to cry out, " I feel that the Lord is here." During such a season as this, one of the sisters who had been anointed to be a prophetess, and was engaged in the turning exercise, was led by the Second eldress to my wife Mary, who was seated at that end of the Hall, and under much exercise of body, in bowing, and twisting, which is their custom, and with closed eyes, and solemn voice proclaimed to her, " You are safe. You will never leave the people of God. For I behold the angels of God encircle you, and their wings meet over your head." I afterwards inquired of this sister about this gift. She said in answer to my questions, that she really saw those Spirits, or angels, and that their dress was like that of the brethren. That is, they wore the Shaker habiliments. That their dress seemed to be of a downy, or velvet material, very beautiful. That with their outstretched wings they formed a complete circle around her, the wing of each touching that of the other. This seemed to be done to protect her against the influences of the world.

At the close of this meeting, as we passed out of the Hall, another of the inspired sisters approached Mary, and addressed her as follows. "*Is it possible!* IS IT POSSIBLE! *that you are gathered into the fold of God! why, I used to know you when I was in the world.*" But this speech will be unintelligible to the reader without the explanation which we afterwards received of it. The inspired sister was at the time possessed of the spirit of some person o Mary's former acquaintance, but who had departed this life, and had joined the Spirit Shakers in the Spirit world. It was this Spirit who addressed Mary through the sister.

This course was designed and calculated to affect the mind of Mary, and force upon her their superstition. And it was not wholly without its effect. It is not uncommon for them to pursue this course with those strangers whom they wish to proselyte, or convert to Shakerism. It is *management*. And such management has been common with other denominations to accomplish the same end, in their protracted meetings, Camp-meetings, Conference-meetings, &c.

The Mountain Meetings.

Every society in this denomination has a place for meeting in the open air, usually at some little distance from their village. Where they assemble twice in the year, and sometimes oftener. These meetings are very curious, and at them this people manifest many of their excentricities, and have many wonderful revelations.

About the year 1841, or—42, a very important revelation was received at the " head of influence," (New-Lebanon) requiring every society in God's Zion upon earth, (the Shakers,) to prepare a place upon some mountain, or hill, in its vicinity, for a Holy place of worship. The place was pointed out to their prophets by inspiration. I will describe the one belonging to the society where we were, as this is the only one I have seen. Doubtless all the others are very similar to this, and were fashioned after one description. They were the conception of one mind, doubtless: Philemon Stewart, the great prophet at the head of influence, was that mind.

The place pointed out for our society was about a mile and a half from our village upon the top of a mountain, and is named Mount Sinai. It is in sight of the mountain chosen for their meeting ground, by the society at New Lebanon, called Mt. Lebanon. But they are too far distant from each other for any verbal communication to pass from one to the other; there being a great gulf, or valley between them. The mountain was named Mount Sinai, after Divine revelation had designated the spot. The brethren went to work and removed the trees and their roots, the stones and other rubbish, smoothed and prepared the ground. It is now covered with a greensward, and surrounded with a plain strip-fence, painted white. It is in the form of a square, and contains I should judge about 3-8ths of an acre. Near the centre is a little spot, enclosed with a fence of a single strip, about fifteen inches high, in form a hexagon. It is called " the Fountain." At the north end of the fountain is erected a marble slab 3 1-2 or 4 feet high. On the north, or outer side of this stone is engraved the following :

Inscriptions on the Monument.
" WRITTEN AND PLACED HERE
By the command of our Lord and Savior Jesus Christ.
THE LORD'S STONE.
Erected upon this Mt. Sinai, May 4th, 1843."
" ENGRAVED AT HANCOCK."
On the south, or side inward to the Fountain, is engraved as follows :
" THE WORD OF THE LORD."
" HERE IS MY HOLY FOUNTAIN,
WHICH I HAVE PLACED HERE,
For the healing of the Nations, who shall here seek my favor.

"And I command all people who shall come to this fountain, not to step within this enclosure, nor place their hands upon this Stone, while they are polluted with sin. I am God the Almighty in whose hands are judgment and mercy. And I will cause my judgments to fall upon the wilful violator of my commands in my own time according to wisdom and truth, whether in this world, or in eternity. For I have created all souls, and unto me they are accountable.

"FEAR YE THE LORD."

There is also, a building erected at the north side of the ground with two apartments, or sitting rooms, one for the sisters, and the other for the brethren. But the fountain claims our particular notice. It is a fountain not of literal waters, but of the water of life, and is exceedingly productive of spiritual gifts. It serves also, as a centre, around which they march, and dance, and sing, and play.

The Heavenly Dress for the Occasion.

The day for meeting upon this mountain, is with the Shakers, a glorious day, a day of rejoicing, and a feast of fat things. All are elated with the idea of going on to the mountain; both old, and young, seem equally elated, all go who are able to walk, and some who are not able to walk, ride, though it is a steep and difficult way for horses and carriages. On this day, the brethren, and sisters wear their usual Sunday clothes, and in addition a most splendid Spiritual dress. This dress cannot be seen by the natural eye, but is described by the Seers, who can see Spiritual things. The dress consisted of a little coat, or tunic, with buttons of gold, and enriched in the most beautiful manner, with gold trimmings; and all the other parts of a full dress to match it. This is the idea I got of the dress from a description of it by one of the sisters. It was received before I went among the people, yet I had the honor of wearing it when attending the mountain meetings. On the evening before, or early on the morning of the day of the meetiug, each family in the society assembles itself in its meeting-room to receive these garments. It is said there is a suit for every one who is worthy, to attend the meeting. Not only one society, of every society throughout the denomination. Every society has its chest of this spiritual clothing. That for our society, was given at Enfield, Ct., and brought home by our ministry. Some of the inspired ones at Enfield, saw the angels bring this box, or chest, into the room, where it was to be received, set it down, and retire. Here the "gifted ones" received, and delivered to the ministry, who brought it away. In doing this, the ministry go through the same motions, and exercises, that they would if a literal chest were in hand. The chest and clothing is kept by the ministry at their shops, where the elders regularly repair before the mountain meeting, and receive a sufficient quantity for their families; return home, assemble their families, and deal it out in the following form. Being assembled in the meeting-room, the elders standing near one end of the hall, and the eldresses near the other end, two brethren at a time approach, and kneel down before the elders, and while remaining in this position, the elders continue to motion with their hands as though tossing something towards them. And it is said, two little angels standing by receive the dresses, and clothe the subjects. And so we are clothed for the morrow. No provision is made to lay off this spiritual dress when we retire, though we take off the literal one. After the meeting is over, the next day we again assemble and return these dresses to the elders in the same form as we received them, viz., by kneeling before the elders, who extend their hands to receive, while the two little angels take off the clothes, and return them into the elder's hands who carry them back to the ministry. It is said that in one instance, one of the Seers, in folding, and laying this clothing into the chest, counted the garments, and one suit was missing. The fact was, one of the sisters failed to return hers with the rest, being engaged at the time about some domestic affairs. Now does not this prove the thing to be a reality? All this formality is gone through with in seriousness and solemnity.

Imagine yourself a Seer, beholding this army of Shakers, glittering in the full splendor of this glorious uniform, winding up the mountain. Is not it a most brilliant sight to behold? None but the eye of the prophet and prophetess can see the uniform. (I understand they have not used this uniform since I left them. What the ministry have done with it I know not, it was left in their keeping.) These mountain meetings are kept as secret from the world as possible, for they feel embarrassed, and annoyed by the presence of spectators. But since we have presumed to place our eyes upon them in their heavenly uniform, we will follow them in their perambulations up the mountain, though we see nothing upon them but their usual Sunday dress. The fashion of dress worn by dandies about sixty years ago. A broad-brimmed drab hat; a strait drab coat; drab vest, very deep, or long waisted, ornamented behind with flaps, or frills, and without a collar; butternut-colored pantaloons; their hair, and beards, all combed and trimmed precisely alike, according to the divine order. This is the dress of the brethren. Though there is some variety now; some of the brethren wear loose frocks. The handsome frocks are made of unfulled cloth, the warp of which is cotton, colored blue, the filling worsted, colored red, making the cloth a changeable color. The handsome pantaloons, for summer are of cotton cloth, with a small blue stripe. The sisters are in the rear of the army, with their long sugar-scoopshaped, palm-leaf bonnets, with silk, or cambric capes to them of various colors; their strait, clean, and nice caps, strait dresses of various colors; some with small blue stripe, some of the changeable cotton and worsted, and every one with a long checked apron, or pinner.

Thus uniformed, and marshalled into regular order, we behold them winding up the mountain. When about a third part of the way up, we come to the forest, and enter a grove of thrifty walnut trees, called "Walnut Grove." Here they halt in a circle, the elders and eldresses at the upper end of the grove, the sisters on their right, and brethren on their left; the lower end of each wing coming round in front so as to form a circle, or rather an ellipsis. The meeting which I have particularly in mind was the first mountain meeting held after I went among the people. It was in May, 1843. We are now in Walnut-Grove. The church family for some reason unknown to me did not meet with us on this day. Yet it was thought necessary that their principal prophetesses should join us, and take the conduct of the meeting. These were Joseph Wicker, the Second elder, Joseph Patten, and Simon Maybee, the two Deacons, and Martha Vanvalin, and Judith Collins, two anointed Seers or prophetesses. Br. Grove, and sister Dana, of the ministry, were also present. But Grove being a diffident man, the management of the meeting fell upon Joseph Wicker. There was also present at this meeting a gentleman from the City of N. Y. Eliezer Parmley: who came as a friend of Robert White, and with Robert. Robert became a member of the Shaker fraternity about this time. I shall speak of him again in this work. The Shakers thought very highly of Mr. Parmly, (and no doubt with good reason) and were very anxious to convert him to Shakerism. No pains were spared to bring him over to the faith. There was always much excitement and preparation when they expected Eliezer, or as they pronounce it, Leezer. They call every body by their christian name. They had many gifts, and revelations, for Leezer. They believed him to be rich, as well as intellectual and refined. They would have considered him a great acquisition.

But to return to the meeting. Joseph Wicker seems to feel that he must entertain the meeting. He comes forth from the rest, and is within the ring ; bowing, and twisting his body in various directions, his eyes and lips in rapid motion, muttering to himself. This is to signify, that he is under the influence of inspiration. Or, as they term it, he is " under operations." Directly he breaks out in an extemporaneous song. Now, Joseph is naturally a very good looking man, a man of more than ordinary abilities, and has a better education than any other one in the society to which he belongs. And he is supposed by them to be the chief among their prophets. After he has concluded his song, sister Dana makes some remarks; and asserts that she knows positively, that the song which has just been sung, was never sung before. That she knows it came directly from heaven." She being of the ministry, her words are received as infallibly correct. But this testimony was designed specially for the benefit of those who were not fully converted. And many declare, " The Lord is here." " Yea, I feel that the Lord is here." And a general excitement seems to pervade the meeting. Various are the operations with which those are seized who are easily wrought upon. Twisting, jerking, bowing, trembling, &c. One sister now appears within the ring turning round as rapidly as the roughness of the ground will allow her to, and, as she turns she moves gradually towards the lower end of the ring; she has a revelation for Leezer. See, as she ceases turning, she is taken with a mighty bowing; bringing her face oftentimes nearly to the grouud; and motioning with her right hand in a very strange and mysterious manner; as she comes near to Mr. Parmley, she does not look up, but bending herself very low, keeping her eyes upon the ground, she begins to talk to him in a very solemn manner. Mr. Parmley seems to be aware that the address is meant for him. And to be approached, and addressed, in such a curious manner, by an entire stranger, a female, in a public assembly, who are all looking on with wonderful interest. Every thing is so strange, mysterious, and unaccountable, that the man is confounded, and covers his face with his hands in confusion. But the prophetess having delivered her message, whirls back again to her place. Joseph Wicker, continues under operations, and now approaches one of the brethren, Franklin Wright. Franklin, is a most excellent brother, and devotes himself unreservedly to build up the cause, and is often under operations. In the world he would be thought a simpleton, but here he is a man of considerable consequence. Joseph walks up to Franklin, holding his hand as though it contained a tumbler, or footglass. Franklin, understanding the play, held out *his* imaginary glass, and Joseph poured the contents of his glass into Franklin's telling him to drink it; it will do you good; it will throw you down; but you will get over it again. So Franklin put his glass to his lips, and emptied it. He immediately began to stagger about like a drunken man; and finally fell down. But he got over it again, as the prophet told him he would. In a few minutes he was on his feet again.

After about a half an hour spent in this way, we take up our march to the mountain top. When we come within a short distance of the meeting-ground, we are required to halt, and in concert *make seven low bows*. After which we are permitted to march on to the ground. This is consecrated ground, and no world's man, no one who has not confessed his sins before God's witnesses, the elders, is allowed within this enclosure. So Mr. Parmley, attended by his friend Robert White, and Nathan Holland, one of the office Deacons, remained outside with other spectators. But he was not forgotten by those within. The prophet Joseph approached him under operations, and delivered to him an inspired message. But his conduct was so strange; his address was so abrupt, his motions so singular, that Mr. Parmley was again obliged to cover his eyes with his hand in his embarrassment.

These meetings on the mountain are designed to be very free and lively, and, also very impressive. It is a time for the special outpouring of Spiritual gifts. I shall be able to describe only a few of these as specimens. They have but little of the regular marching, and dancing, at these meetings. Some preaching, exhortation, singing, dancing, marching, whirling, shaking, prophesying, talking in unknown languages, &c. But the principal part of the time is taken up in such gifts, as I will describe.

Some leading member says, the brethren, and sisters, are required to go to the fountain and bathe. They will find sponges in the fountain; and towels, by the side of the fountain. (The fountain has already been discribed.) So all approach the fountain as opportunity offers, the brethren at one side, and sisters at the other. And go through with all the motions which would be made if actually bathing in water. They even turn to and scrub one another. But there is not literally either towel, sponge, or water. This ceremony over, some one of the Seers has another gift.

There is in the fountain some pocket-handkerchiefs, for the brethren, and sisters. Every one approaches, and makes the motion to take up a handkerchief. I suppose spiritual water will not wet spiritual handkerchiefs. Joseph says, "we know not what the word will be for us to do next. The Spirit will tell us what to do." And after waiting a few minutes, he says, "the word is to *leap!* let us *leap*." Then every one, both old and young, male and female, jumps up as high as he is able, two or three times. After a little season, he says, "The word is, to go forth and sow. There is by the fountain a measure of seed, to be sown, and a vessel of water, with which to water the ground. The vessel of water to be placed and carried upon the left shoulder, while we sow the seed." So we pass through the motion of shouldering our water, take up our measure of seed, and form ourselves into a column at the north side of the meeting ground, facing the South ; and in concert begin to swing our hands, as in the act of sowing. We all move forward and sow as we march across the meeting ground, and beyond till we come to a fence, when we wheel about, take the water from our shoulder, and water the ground as we march back.

In the middle of the day, of the meeting held in the spring of the year, which comes in May, we hold a grand feast. I do not know the origin, or object of this feast; but will endeavor to describe it.

Two rows of benches are arranged for seats, a few feet apart, upon which the brethren, and sisters, seat themselves, facing inward, and imagine a table before them. The brethren sit at one table, and the sisters at another. The seats are literal, but the table, and furniture, are all imaginary, or spiritual.

Those persons who have been anointed to be prophets, and prophetesses, (this anointing has already been described) are sent forth to gather food for the table. So they go out a little distance from the table, the anointed brethren in one direction, and the anointed sisters in another. The brethren shake the trees, and gather the fruit, in baskets, and bring it in upon their shoulders. The trees, and the fruit, and the baskets, are all imaginary; but all the motions are made as if every thing were literal. You may see them stand pulling, and shaking, as though they had hold of a small tree, shaking off the fruit; and now stooping to gather up the fruit, and placing it in the basket, and then tugging at the basket to place it upon the shoulder, and staggering off with it towards the tables, and then distributing it on the tables. Thus they gather apples, pears, lemons, oranges, mellons, &c. All in the month of May, and in this northern climate. But all is spiritual.

The sisters also, in their department, prepare and bring on various dishes. Turkey, chicken, pudding, pies, green corn, and beans, &c. &c. And they lean over to place the varions dishes upon the table. And now see them eat. They seem to use knives and forks, chew and swallow, pass the food from one to the other. And the inspired ones pretended that they could positively see, and taste the different articles of fruit, and food, as really as if they were literal food. They had wine also; and some mimicked the drunken man. There was not the best of order about this feast, notwithstanding, it was directed by inspiration. And the anointed ones waited upon the table. For the dinner, the desert, and the wine, were all partaker of at the same time. After we had partaken of this feast of fat things, we rose up, to retire; but Joseph calls out to us to pay our tithes. The inspired were now seated at the table and we waited on them. That is, the laity waited on the priesthood, and this paid their tithes.

The feast was now ended, and the people rose up to play again. Indeed, the whole of it seemed to be regarded by many of them as mere play. It was as I have heard little children say, " we did'nt eat real food, we only *played* eat." Indeed a Shaker meeting, what they call a real free and lively meeting, is the consummation of all silly actions and speeches. The inspired ones particularly, seem to vie with each other for the mastery in silliness. To see so many people of all ages, from eighty years, down to little children zealously, and with a considerable degree of seriousness practicing all this nonsense; and calling it *inspiration!* is an outrage upon common sense. Before sitting down to the feast described above, all kneel down in solemn devotion around their imaginary table; and also again before retiring from the table. After the feast, the exercises are resumed, and are very much the same as before. I will describe a few more of their gifts, and transcribe a few of their songs. These together with what I have described, will show the character of their meetings on the mountain.

They believe that the spirits of the departed, honor their meetings with their presence. The inspired ones can see them, and hold converse with them. They estimated that 40,000 were present at their mountain meeting at this time, hovering around and looking on with pleasure and approbation. All such spirits are in the Shaker faith, dressed in the Shaker garb, and subject to a government of which theirs is a pattern. The common members there have to get permission of their lead to visit their brethren on the earth, or to enjoy any other privilege. Some one of the sisters often cries out in " a gift" that " Mother Ann is here, O, Mother Ann is here! and desires her love to the brethren and sisters." Sometimes when Mother Ann cannot come, herself, she sends her love by some other spirits. Sometimes it is given out in " bright balls." The inspired one receives these balls of Mother's love, and tosses them out to the brethren, and sisters, who hold out their hands and catch them. It is curious to see the whole assembly hold out theirs to catch these imaginary balls. The faithful ones believe them to be real, though not tangible to their natural senses. Though the inspired ones say they can see them and feel them with their hands. They are about as big as ones fist, white, and bright like clean paper. They are often written upon with some communication to the recipient. Sometimes St. Paul is present, Peter, and others of the apostles. Generals Washington, and Lafayette, were seen on the Lebanon mountain, mounted on their white chargers, with sword in hand guarding the holy mountain.

The spirit of the departed of all nations, and of every language ever spoken under heaven present themselves at times to this people. It is often the case that some one of these spirits enters into the body of a sister, (the brethren seldom have the gifts) who upon this, if she yields to the influence, loses all control over her own body, and the spirit manifests itself through her, talks in its own language, sings, dances its native dances, or quarrels with other spirits of its own nation. Thus in a midst of a solemn meeting a sister may be seen jumping up, and endeavoring to imitate the dance and singing of an Indian chief; how well I could not judge, having never witnessed the performance, by an Indian. Sometimes several of the sisters pretend to be possessed by the native spirits at the same time, and talking gibberish to each other. Sometimes they have a dispute, and a fight, and seem to shoot at each other; when the one shot at actually falls down as if dead.

It seems impossible that any sensible person should be so duped as to believe such trash as this; yet a majority of the members seem candidly and seriously to believe all this to be real possession or inspiration. The second elder in our family, Barnabas Sprague, talked with me about these matters seriously, thinking them unaccountable except they were real.

They do not see the absurdity of these spirits who are so good, so much in union in the heavenly world, as to be permitted to come and possess even the holy and anointed ones among them, *fighting!* so malicious as to strive and kill each other! Is it so, that the shaker community in the spiritual world is composed of such characters? Or was the vision false? And if this vision were false, how shall we know that they are not all false? But I will not discuss this point here. Sure I am that when men begin to think for themselves they must reject such things.

We will return a few moments, to see a few more of the gifts of some of our mountain meetings. At one meeting, the entertainments seemed rather to drag, when the elder turned to one of the inspired sisters and says, "Come Sally aint there some native spirits here? can't we have a native song?" Sally looked very grave and made no reply. Directly there was a gift of spiritual wine, of which they all partook. The eldress carried some to Sally, (there were two sisters, Sally and Mary Smith, I may have mistaken the one for the other, though I think it was Sally) and says, "come Sally, drink a good deal of this, so that you may have a good gift of a song." Sally seemed to drink heartily, and directly began to show the effects of the wine; and sang us a most lively and theatrical song in the Indian tongue, (said to be) dancing at the same time with much vigor and spirit, imitating the Indian dance. Indeed this was an excellent performance, and was highly amusing and entertaining even to those who believed she did it all by her own natural powers. The faithful ones really believed she was actually possessed by a native, that is, an Indian spirit, which spirit was the author of this original and extemporaneous song, the tune and the dancing. The fact is, Sally was herself a smart girl, a good singer, and a good dancer. She was capable of originating this whole performance. I cannot give the song which she sung at this time; probably it was never written out and perhaps never sung afterwards. But I will here give one which if I am not mistaken was sung in a similar manner, on a similar occasion, by the same author. And if as well performed, doubtless was equal to the one of which I have spoken. Here it is.

> Te he, te how, te hoot, te te hoot,
> Me be Mother's pretty pappose,
> Me ting, me dant, te I diddle um,
> Because me here to whities come,
> He di diddy, ti diddle O;
> Round, around, and round me go,
> Me leap, me jump, e up and down,
> On good whity, shiny ground.

When reading this song it appears very silly, but being well performed it was quite theatrical; it was as good as any part of the meeting. Another gift was this, John Valin an inspired brother, who lives at the "North House," says, "There is a bowl of *love* and *union* for the brethren and sisters, it stands at the head of the fountain, and there is but one spoon in the bowl. Every brother and sister must come forward and take a spoonful or lose their union." So they began to march up one at a time to get their love and union. The bowl and spoon were imaginary, the form of eating was as one eats bread and milk. The most simple and true were the first who eagerly press forward to obtain their love and union. But this was evidently going to be a tedious affair, for the whole meeting to come up one at a time and eat his spoonful. The leading elder perceiving this, gave a witty turn to the matter. Now this elder is a witty old man, and in his "nateral creation" (as they express it) a jolly fat man. With a very arch look at the leading sisters who stood near him, he very pertly says, "I don't know about this spoon business. It will take all day to get through with it, come, come up and get your love and union; there is more than one spoon there I know." This John, the author of the gift is a good simple brother, and did not foresee what a tedious gift he was imposing upon the brethren and sisters.

There is a fact concerning this John's conversion, which I must relate as it was related to me by one of the brethren, in whose veracity and unwavering faith in shakerism I have not the least doubt. When John first came among the people, he boldly derided the reality of the gifts; and he went so far as to say, the sisters need not think to deceive him by tumbling down and kicking up their heels in meeting, he did not believe a word of it." For it is believed that they are taken by the spirits and thrown down against their will; sometimes persons are pulled and jerked around with great violence, and made to tremble and shake against their will. Well, this John, after this hard hearted unbelief and opposition to "the way and work of God," as he was returning home from meeting one Sabbath, he was seized by the spirits, and repeatedly thrown down, pulled out of his course, and his progress so interrupted that it was with the greatest exertions, and a very long time before he reached his home. Since that time he has been a good believer in all the gifts and revelations approved of by the elders. This was told me by that good brother to convince me of the reality of such things.

The reality of the case was probably this. He had lost much union, and was likely to lose his connexion with this people by his opposition. It was necessary for him to regain his union; and he took this the only way in which he could do so the most effectually. Very many are driven into this humbuggery in a similar way.

Martha Van Valen, the natural sister of this John, seems to be the principal prophetess in the church order in this society. She figures as the instrument in some of the most important revelations yet to be recorded. She came forward near the close of one of the meetings upon the mountain, and among other visions, she said there was raised upon a very tall pol an ensign or banner, printed all over in large letter of various colors. She called upon the seers, to say if they beheld it. Several of them responded, yea. And they named many of the colors. She said she could not read or explain the writing upon this ensign at this time; but it would be read and explained at another time; perhaps at the next meeting. But I never heard that any thing was said of it afterwards. When they were naming the colors, one saw green, another red, another blue, &c. One saw black; yea, said several others, they are black! This signified that something dreadful was approaching.

Besides these general gifts, they often have revelations for individuals, especially for " young believers," as they call those who have been with them but a short time, to encourage them in the Shaker travel. At one of the mountain meetings, I was led up to the head of the fountain and placed by the side of Robert White, another young believer to receive a gift. When I returned home from the meeting I made the following record of it, which I here transcribe.

"It was delivered to us by the prophetess Martha V. V. She said it was a present from the blessed Savior. My gift was a beautiful white box, in which was a bright gold leaf, and on the leaf was written the word of the eternal God for me to speak to his beloved children, (the shakers) and to those who know not the way of salvation. So according to the prediction I was to be a shaker preacher. Brother Robert's gift was also a beautiful white box, and within it a gold leaf, on which was written something (which I do not recollect.) In addition to this, he received a beautiful garment, and a trumpet. The Savior desired us to receive these presents with his love. We said politely to the Instrument, Martha, that we were thankful for our presents; and she assured us that we were welcome."

Robert White came among the shakers about the time I went there. He was formerly a quaker, and wore the quaker garb when he came there. He is a man I should judge, of about fifty-five or sixty years of age; of more than usual intelligence and refinement, and seems to have an excellent heart. Formerly a merchant in the city of N. Y. and more recently a farmer in N. J.; I think in the town of Shrewsbury. He is supposed by the Shakers to be worth about thirty thousand dollars. A man of good intelligence, good heart, and thirty thousand dollars is no small acquisition. And the way they flatter him is a caution. I have been astonished to see him swallow it down, but flattery blinds the eyes amazingly. It was so fulsome and so palpable, as one of the brethren who is in good union, said to me, "I tell them Robert is a big fish; and they have to bait differently to catch great fish, from what they do to catch little fishes." But a fish when first caught is very slippery.

But I must return once more to the mountain gifts. At the first meeting held on the mountain, there was a revelation given to every individual who attended the meeting. It was given in the form of a little book. The individual who received the gift could not see or sense it in any way until it was transcribed by some one of the visionists or prophets. I will merely transcribe one of these books as a specimen. It is short.

The following is a literal transcript of the original. The subject of it, Benjamin Collins, is above seventy years of age, and a most thorough and devout shaker. But before he was converted to shakerism, he was the husband of his second wife, and the father of eighteen children. He regards this little book as a rich treasure, literally sent him by Mother Ann. He loaned it to me to read, and I privately copied it. Here it is.

Specimens of Written Revelations

Given on the Mountain when the first Meeting was held there.

"*The following communication is a book given by the prophet Elijah, on Mount Sinai, Sept.* 18—*to Benjamin Collins. Written Feb.* 27*th*, 1843."

"Beloved brother and fellow traveller in the gospel; (for so I address you) receive this communication with my love and blessing, which I now give unto you as a token of remembrance, for your faithfulness in well doing. You have lived to see the day which has long been predicted, a day when Christ has made his second appearing, the latter day of glory; and have been called and chose to be a rightful heir of his kingdom, though you was called at the eleventh hour of the day. If you continue faithful to the end, great will be your reward in heaven. The prophets of old longed to see this day; but died without the sight. Dear brother, the day is fast hastening, when you will be called home to receive the reward of your doings. You have lived to see the work of God increase and go on in a marvellous manner, but a still greater work is at hand, when God will shake the heavens and the earth, and the inhabitants thereof, but you will not live to see much further increase in the body."

"So be ye now prepared to go,
And leave all earthly things below,
Unto your treasure house that is in store
Laid up for you when time's no more.

O be not slack to hasten on,
The time will come when you are gone,
That you will see these things fulfilled,
And labor in the gospel field.

And with the reapers will go out
To reap the earth, then you will shout
To see the glorious work go on,
That in your day has now begun.

Now while you live do all you can
To slay and conquer the old man;
For every step you take while here
Will make your crown shine brighter there.

So with new courage, faith and zeal,
Press on your way, then you may feel
My love and blessing as you go,
To comfort and to strengthen you.

With these few lines you may receive
The love of all your heavenly lead,
Here our good Mother Ann has closed
Her blessing and a pure white rose,

For to be given unto you,
To help you on, to bear you through;
And Father William doth bestow
A pair of shoes white as the snow,

For you to wear when you go home,
And join the pure angelic throng.
So fare you well in love and peace
And let these lines your love increase.
Gotten by Lovisa Patten."

This book, or communication, professes to have been written and sent by the prophet Elijah; not on material paper, but spiritual. It was not therefore tangible to any of the natural senses. Benjamin Collins could not see it, until the prophetess or visionist Lovisa had transcribed it upon material paper. I took the liberty to punctuate the work, and introduce the capital letters in the prose. I made no other correction. One would naturally think that one of the prophet Elijah's age and experience ought to be able to punctuate his own writing, use the capitals correctly, and write grammatically. But as neither is done in the above communication, it is but just to conclude it is not his. It is derogatory to his character to attribute it to him. The verses also are not poetry, but miserable doggerrell. Can the elders believe that the prophet Elijah was guilty of originating the above communication? No intelligent person can believe it. It is most evidently the production of an ignorant and weak mind. It is the fact with all or nearly all their pretended revelations. The instrument through whom it is pretended they are revealed, is most plainly the author. The revelation is the production of his own mind. But if the brethren and sisters believe it is from God, the elders can make use of it to enforce obedience, and they do it. I will give another specimen.

> My child now lend a listening ear
>   Unto thy mother's voice;
> I've heard thy sighs, I've seen thy tears,
>   And now I say rejoice.
>
> And read this little book I've sent,
>   Of peace and consolation,
> That you may feel your mother's love
>   In the midst of tribulation.
>
> You've much to suffer, much to bear,
>   In body here I know,
> But if you're faithful you shall share
>   My blessing as you go.

Be wise my child in all your way,
   Be careful what you speak,
Be on your guard both night and day,
   And labor to be meek.

And then my love and blessing too,
   Shall ever rest on thee,
Sweet peace and consolation shall
   Your true companion be.

To help you on your journey through,
   To comfort you while here,
And when you're done with time below,
   Your spirit it will cheer.

I have a mansion now prepared,
   Where you will take a seat,
And in my Father's kingdom share
   His glory that's complete.

Beyond this vale of pain and woe
   Where you can take your rest,
Where peace and consolation flow
   Among the pure and just.

So now be comforted my child,
   For you are not forgot,
The holy angels on you smile,
   When you do fear your God.

And they will waft your spirit home,
   When you are called to go,
And guard your body to the tomb,
   And guide you safely home.

   From Job of old to Samuel Robinson. Written Jan. 18, 1843.

   I give the following because it is Mother Ann's poetry.

"*A gold leaf from Mother Ann.—Instrument, Jane Osborn.*

" With a bright leaf of gold I've come,
With cheering words right from my home,
With love that's pure, with love that's meek,
These words I unto you will speak.

My friend and child I now do say,
Don't never cease to watch and pray,
Don't keep your sword which is so bright,
Within its sheath and out of sight.

For this you oft should try to use,
This will the serpent badly bruise,
And all who stand on gospel ground,
Should their shrill trumpets loudly sound.

O be encouraged now I say;
If you do strive from day to day,
To walk the little narrow road,
You shall in heaven find an abode.

Of heavenly food you'll daily eat,
And worship with your hands and feet;
You'll sing forth praises to your God,
That you this blessed path have trod.

My little dove I often send,
To cheer your heart O my dear friend;
Some soothing spirit oft you feel,
Yea, often this a wound will heal.

Try to be watchful evermore,
This will increase your gospel store;
Think that your guardian spirit's near,
This will instill a holy fear.

Infirmities are creeping on,
Your life and vigor's almost done,
Soon you will launch an endless shore,
Where sickness, pain and death's no more.

When once your spirit is set free,
From earthly things you're called to be,
You'll bless the Lord, to him you'll bow,
And from your lips sweet songs will flow.
So farewell."
" Written Feb. 26, 1843. For Samuel Robinson."

These communications from the spiritual world, were given by the spirits at the Sept. meeting, but were not transcribed until the date they bear. Being a spiritual book, could not be seen by natural eyes until transcribed by some one of the Seers. The reader will probably think the above specimens of doggerell rhyme do not do much credit to Mother Ann as a poetess, or the prophet Elijah and father Job as poets. As to mother Ann, there is no doubt that she lived and died an ignorant woman; and I know not but she remains ignorant to this day, and may be the author of such trash as is attributed to her. But compare the one attributed to Job, with that of his in the old testament. The ancient poem which he wrote while on earth, is indeed sublime poetry. That which Lovisa Patten attributes to him in these latter days, is most wretched doggerell. A critical mind cannot avoid seeing the imposition. And it is so with nearly all their revelations. They show upon the face of them that they are false. But the Shakers have some better poetry than the specimens I have given. They will be inclined to ask me why I do not give their best pieces. The reason is, I wish to give a fair specimen, and the pieces I have given are better than their poetry will average. If they have better poetry, they have also much that is worse. Their communications are always characteristic not of the spirit which reveals them, but of the person or instrument through whom they are revealed. Ungrammatical, badly spelt, without punctuation, meagre in style, contracted in sentiment. But if it be given through a person of brilliant talents, the communication will be proportionably elevated. For instance, if father Job gives a communication through Jo Wicker (as he is familiarly called) and another through Lovisa Patten or Sarah Smith, the two pieces would differ very materially in real merit, in grammatical construction, in spelling, in punctuation, in every thing. Even if the pieces be written out as the little books given on the mountain, the same discrepancy appears. The article is always characteristic of the instrument through whom it professes to be revealed. It partakes nothing of that spirit from whom it professes to come. This fact is sufficient to convince every candid person that the *instrument is the real author*, and there is no revelation about it.

The reader will be inclined to ask if there is no evidence accompanying the pretended revelation? None except the "operations." That is, the turning, shaking, jerking, bowing, winking, and such like.

These gifts, and revelations, are not confined to the mountain meetings, but are common in all their meetings. I will now give a few specimens of songs, in their unknown tongues. The reader is to bear in mind that all their songs, and all the tunes which they sing, come to them by special revelation.

" O calivin criste I no vole,
Calivin criste liste um,
I no vole vinin ne viste,
I no vole viste vum. N. R."

" Hi con di re ve um si hon lene ve lon O,
Vi nick ane asked on vande sack ane O le,
Mu ne on a ke ve le O hiek ane has ca volon,
Si ne nin a ve ve lom on hi nis ka sen a ke hola.
N. R."

N. R., stands for Nancy Riley, the second eldress, in the gathering order.

Cero vera ascenda hawza monev vale,
Silo vera allura oze vando calise,
Vo lo cali se lou an ni dins vurdo,
O lo va li se me selon mace dan za va.

"Conave van eve va cana vana vo,
Van eke wan awe ve cana vane,
Wan que sana que ve nana vane co,
Sana se fana ve se ol ca nane. S. S."

"O que won wista wa,
We quou quistu ka,
Quo con ristu we,
Wo zon zane ke,
Que wain wisna quo,
Se nain quisna woo,
We sain win no haw,
Ka ween na na wah. S. S."

S. S., stands for Sarah Smith, a young sister, and one of the " Holy anointed."

Some of their inspirations are partly in an unknown tongue, and partly in the English.

"O we will praise our Maker, yea, we even will,
Ki lo vin sa vo van vos onena vil,
Care van se neve cara van sa ve,
I le vin se vo van vos onena va. L. W."

"I lo le viteca vum vole os ca nere von,
I lo le viteca vum se ra os ca nere von,
I le viteca vole vum se ra os ca nere von,
I le viteca vole vum se ra os ca nana. L. W."

The last of these is often sung in their meetings, in a march, as they "labor" or march.

"Selera vane van vo canera van se lava,
Dilera van se lane cinera van se vo,
'Tis Mother's Holy love, love she sent it by her dove dove,
'Twas vene van se vane, 'twill ever more endure."
L. W.

L. W., stands for Loiza Weed. She was a young sister, and one of the " Holy anointed." She has now withdrawn from the Shakers, and is married.

The ministry inform the brethren, and sisters, generally through the elders, that there is a certain gift for them, and then they must all labor for this gift, that is, mentally to be inspired with the gift. For example, the elders inform the brethren and sisters, when assembled in meeting, that " the ministry tell us there is a gift of songs, for us brethren and sisters, now let us every one labor for a song. We must go forth in the *gift*, brethren, and sisters, if we would receive a blessing." So then, for days, or weeks, the brethren and sisters dwell upon the subject. Until some Holy Spirit comes and inspires them with a song; communicating to their minds by impression, or otherwise, the *language*, and the *tune*. And the songs that are brought forth on such occasions are a curiosity. Some of the preceding songs in unknown language, may be specimens of such a gift.

It is noticeable in all the Shaker gifts, and revelations, that the gift whatever it may be, always partakes more or less of the character of the instrument through whom it is manifested. If the instrument be a shallow weak minded person, this quality will also characterize the gift. If an ignorant person, ignorance will be manifested in the gift. If of a strong imagination, the gift will be proportionally brilliant. (See the testimonies of Harriet Goodwin, and Mary Ann Jennings.) If of an original turn of mind, we have something new. There was one aged sister in our family, who was often under operations, and at such times practiced the turning gift, but being a large fleshy woman, she could turn but slowly, and for a short time. But what was peculiar and always attended her gifts, was, her hands were always in continual motion, as if spinning linen on the foot wheel. This labor is still performed among the Shakers, and she has been a very smart spinner Another stamps, rages, and pronounces dreadful judgments, &c., &c.

A few more specimens of the gift of songs.

"I am a little dove just come from above,
With Holy Holy Mother's love and blessing,
I will feed you with crumbs that shall satisfy your soul,
And will give you strength and power."

Another song, which they sing and dance in meeting.

"I am a little bird, I sing complete,
Time the tune with my little feet,
I can dance, and I can hop,
I can shout and wake you up."

"O, here is Mother, O, my brethren do pertake, do pertake with Mother,
O, here is manney, (manna,) free for all freely flows from Mother,
O, my sisters do pertake, do pertake from Mother,
Here is manney, free for all, freely flows from Mother,
I will eat, I will eat, I will eat my full supply, I will eat with Mother,
And I'll sing Holy, Holy, is Mother, and I'll play on the jubilee,
And I'll play on the jubilee, and I'll sing Holy, Holy, is Mother."

They sometimes have a hugging gift. The elder says, "I feel as though I wanted a little gift of hugging." The brethren then gather up into one clump, and the sisters into another, and have a general embrace.

When I have witnessed so many ridiculous things in the private meetings of the Shakers, I have thought it not so very improbable, that the gift of *dancing naked*, might have been practiced by them in the days of "Mother Ann." They were boldly charged with it by many who seceded from them. Haskett in his "Shakerism unmasked" says, of this charge, "It is not gratuitous, but founded upon evidence of the first class, and corroborated by circumstances." But he labors to show that this practice did not arise from any design to gratify the flesh, but rather to mortify and crucify the same. This practice did not in all probability continue for a great length of time. I might quote such gifts, and such songs, from manuscript, and from memory without limit. But my object is only to give such specimens as shall convey an idea of Shakerism as it was exhibited to me. And I verily believe the best side of the system was presented to my view. My first impressions of Shakerism, and while its deformities were kept out of sight, and they were kept from my view as long as practicable, were favorable And while they were so, I was encouraged by the elders to speak in their meetings. And I endeavored to speak in such a way as not to discourage their '*gifts.*' I went so far as to tell them, that I loved to see them act out their feelings, to act freely and without restraint. I always loved a free meeting, &c. The elder told me afterwards that my communications had been construed by the brethren, and sisters, into an acknowledgement of my belief, that these manifestations were what they pretended to be, special revelations from God. And not being willing to be instrumental in carrying on this delusion, and being thoroughly disgusted with the gifts, I felt it a duty to explain my position. Accordingly on Sabbath day, during a season of silence in their meeting, while all were seated, I arose and addressed them briefly, to the following effect.

"That I believe in the revelation of God. In modern as well as ancient revelation. And argued in favor of the latter. And that every one who strove aright for communion with God, was more or less inspired. But it is to be considered, that a revelation to me, is not necessarily a revelation to others. No person is under obligations to believe a thing because it has been revealed to me, unless I can show him convincing evidence that such thing has indeed been revealed from God. Neither am I obliged to receive a thing because another says it has been revealed to him. It may indeed *be* a revelation to him, but it is not therefore a revelation to me; neither am I bound to believe it on his testimony. If the thing be revealed to me by the Spirit, I know it to be true from the testimony of the Spirit, but if it be revealed to another, I cannot receive it without external proof.

We are liable to be deceived about these things. If indeed, a person has once been supernaturally inspired, and has received a special revelation from God, it does not follow that the person is ever after infallible. He may afterwards think he is inspired when he is not. We all know that this is a very common error. People very often sincerely mistake their own imaginations for revelations of God.

In view, then, of these reasons, and facts, I feel under no obligations to believe all that professes to be revelation. I believe in both ancient, and modern revelation, but do not believe all that professes to be revelation.

I believe also, that *simplicity* is a very important requisite in the Christian character. We all ought to be simple, and plain, in our intercourse, and conduct. There is a distinction to he made, however, between simplicity, and silliness. Silliness is folly, an approach to foolishness. But simplicity is a manifestation of true wisdom ; and is consistent with profound dignity. Our Savior is an example to us of perfect simplicity. He was always simple, and always dignified; but never silly. He was always calm, and considerate, knowing perfectly well what he was about to say and do. Adapting his language to the capacities of all, without pride, or haughtiness, and without affectation. He told the simple truth in the most simple and intelligible manner!"

This speech was the death blow to my union. The young people were privately cautioned against such sentiments, and such preaching; and warned against me as a dangerous man. When I observed this coldness of manner towards me, I questioned the elder as to the reason of it. He reluctantly admitted that it was in consequence of my remarks at the meeting-house. The particular remarks to which exception was made, were, first, " I said there was a difference between simplicity and silliness." The remark was admitted to be true in itself, but was thought to have an application to the " gifts" of the young sisters. They thought I had designed to tell them they were silly. This of course, I denied. I had no such design. And, indeed, I did not think they would make this direct application of it to themselves.

The elder said, these things would appear silly to the natural mind. And, if the sisters did these things of themselves, *it would be silly!* And so the subject seems to be viewed. Actions which when performed by human beings in their own powers, are contemptibly silly, if performed by an angel, or a Holy Spirit, are commendable and dignified. An angel may take possession of a human body, and perform all manner of antics ; roll in the mud, bark like a dog, crow like a rooster, &c., and this would not be silly because performed by the Spirit saint, or angel. I confess I cannot feel the force of such logic. The very fact that these things, or "gifts," are silly, is evidence to me that they are human and not Divine.

The other remark objected to by the elder, was, "I said our Savior, always knew perfectly well what he was about to do, or say." This was supposed to militate against the "gifts," as the brethren, and sisters, when under operations of the Spirit, do not pretend always to know what they do and say; but yielding themselves up to the influence of the Spirit, lose their own consciousness, and the Spirit possessing them, only manifests itself. This I doubt not, is in many cases a real delusion.

The ministry do not usually attend the meetings of the common members, but having their dwelling over the meeting room of the families, they have invented a way of their own to observe the meetings, and not be observed themselves. The two flights of stairs, by which they ascend into their dwelling, are at either end of the meeting room. The sisters' stairs at one end, and the brethren's at the other. These stairs are ceiled up with boards; and a door communicates with each flight of stairs from the meeting room. Each member of the minstry has a hole bored through the ceiling of the stairway ; and coming cautiously, and silently, part way down the stairs, seats himself against his auger hole, and peeping through, observes the meeting at his leisure.

AMONG THE SHAKERS.   85

The Whirling Gift.

FEB. 23, 1845.

Meeting to-day at the meeting-house. A *free* and *lively* meeting. Commenced as usual by singing. Many singers, sing loud, lively tunes, but there is very little melody, or harmony in the singing. Speaking by David Terry. He hoped every one, brethren and sisters, has " sot" out determined to persevere in the way of God. Every one has got a work to perform. " Taint" something that we can begin and labor a little while, and then leave off; but we've got to labor for it. Every one has got to strive for one. So I hope brethren and sisters, we shall every one labor to become zealous in every good work. Labor to come to the truth. The truth is worth more than all the news, and all the great histories, and all of every thing that has ever been printed, by human hand. So brethren, and sisters, I hope we may be able to make some gain in the good things of the Spirit.

Elder Br. Reuben said, brethren and sisters, I hope we shall labor to treasure up what has been spoken; I believe it is the truth. I feel happy to meet so many of my brethren and sisters here to-day, to worship God in the Spirit. I think the brethren and sisters have shown a good deal of zeal to come out to meeting at so inclement a time. I can truly say I feel thankfnl for the privilege of meeting with my brethren and sisters. It does us good to meet together. I felt as though I wanted to assemble together with my brethren and sisters, to worship God. It has been some time since we have met together. When we don't meet together for some time we are apt to grow cold. When we assemble together we can strengthen each other and increase each others zeal. So I hope that when we go forth we shall go forth with zeal and energy, brethren and sisters. We can go forth in the travel manner.

The singers, about six or eight or more of them, then placed themselves in the center of the room, in two ranks, the one facing the other, sisters facing sisters, and brethren facing brethren, with the spit box in the middle. And the remainder formed a circle around them, three abreast. The brethren by themselves, forming one segment of the circle, and the sisters by themselves forming the other. The children form the inside file of the circle. The singers then strike up a march, which they sing over four or five times, repeating once, each part of the tune, every time; while the company march, and all, both singers and laborers beat the time with their hands. Each placing his two hands before him in a horizontal direction moves them up and down in time with the tune. When the tune ceases all stop until another tune is struck. After a few tunes in this way, elder brother says, the brethren and sisters may take their places to go forth in the quick manner.

They then took their places; the sisters in the east part of the hall, and the brethren in the west, leaving a space between. There is not much regularity to this dance. Except that the singers form a line in front of a seat which runs east and west on the north side of the hall, standing about middle way. The company stand facing the singers, the elders being in front, and nearest the middle of the hall from east to west. When a tune is struck up, they turn, the brethren to the left, and sisters to the right, and perform a sort of trotting step, each company around its own division of the room until the set of the tune, when all turn facing the singers and shuffle. This continues for about three minutes: when there is a respite for a half of a minute, or a minute. And another tune is struck. At the intervals of the tunes, there is sometimes speaking. Some brother, or sister, expresses their thankfulness for their privilege in the Gospel, and express their determination to be obedient to their beloved elders, and keep the way of God. Sometimes the elders exhort the brethren and sisters to be zealous, and labor for the "gifts and power of God." In these exhortations, the elders manifest great zeal, and energy themselves.

As these exercises continue, the zeal increases, the whole company frequently clap their hands in concert. Some begin to turn round with great rapidity, some leap, and shout, throw up their hands, and perform all manner of gesticulations, talk in unknown togues, sing in unknown tongues. Sometimes, as to-day, for instance, two or three times, all join in one concert of yelling, screaming, shouting, shaking, with all their might, thumping their feet upon the floor, with great rapidity, altogether presenting a scene, and making a noise which cannot be described. Should a stranger come in at this moment, he must think it a perfect bedlam; and would probably be frightened nearly out of his wits. When the din is not so great that one cannot be heard, there is preaching, prophesying, speaking in unknown togues, and singing songs by special inspiration. All this time the young sisters continue their turning so swiftly, that the air gathering under their garments, raises them so as to expose their red petticoats, and other under clothes, and even the fastening of their hose, and sometimes when their clothes happen to brush against a sister near them, it exposes their persons still more. But they must not be checked in their gifts, for it is by the inspiration of God, that all these things are done. They often fall prostrate upon the floor, and all animation seems lost for a season. There is frequently with them a crouching, and bowing, as though affected with a shock of electricity.

When one ceases turning, she frequently embraces with her arms, another sister, and continues crouching, and bowing, for some time, and seems to have a special gift for that sister. One who has had the gift of turning in a high degree, assured us they did this because they were too dizzy to stand up alone. Others who have been gifted, have assured me, that this is the reason why they fall down. They cannot stand for dizziness. And that all their skill in turning is acquired by practice.

All their meetings are not carried to the same excess as the one which I have described above. And never have I known them to have a meeting which made any comparison with this, when any spectators are present from the worlds; a these are sometimes allowed to attend our meetings at home in the gathering family. None are permitted to attend our meetings at the meeting-house, since 1837, when this revival commenced. Some who have been here since that time, assure me, that the meeting I witnessed to-day, would not begin to compare with the meetings they had in the commencement of the revival. In the commencement of the revival, many went into the turning who were unaccustomed to turning; consequently they would frequently fall down; become sick and vomit. Some would go out, others run to the spit-box; some of the younger portion even bedaubed the floor.

In the meeting to-day, before it had come to its height of excitement, and interest. David Terry, who had visited the society, at Enfield, spoke of his visit; and of the beautiful gifts they had there. I have got some love for you, I am going to give it out by and by. He said the children there had given up all their plays; it was found to be just as well for them to have some useful employment. Work answered every purpose of play. They had not been seen to slide down hill once this winter, nor to snow-ball. After laboring a few tunes more, he came forward to give out the spiritual presents which he had brought from Enfield. He had six baskets, three upon each arm, filled with love, fruit, and other good things. Some of these gifts were from the people at Enfield, and some from Mother Ann and others, in the spiritual world. These presents were accompanied by attending angels. All, both angels and presents and baskets, were invisible to all, except the Seers. So David, after informing us what he had got for us, and of the angels in attendance, steps up to the invisible altar in the space between the brethren and sisters, with his six invisible baskets, loaded with invisible love, wine, fruit, gold chains, &c. And being a very awkward man, he made most woful work in delivering himself of his burden. He could set down but one basket at a time. And it took him a long minute to set them all down, and the grotesque figures he made with his arm, and body were truly ridiculous. Then the whole audience walked up in irregular order, to receive each a gold chain, and made the same motion as if taking one from the basket, and put around the neck. " Now, (says elder brother,) I want every one should do just as though you could see and sense the reality there. For it is just as real as though you could see it with your natural eyes. So when we had received each, the gold chain, we all turned round four times and shouted each time. We then walked up again, and helped ourselves, each, to a bottle of wine, and made the motion to drink it. Then turned round four times again and clapped our hands each time. It being required by those who sent the gifts, that they should be received in this manner. After this, David Terry said, " There is one gift I had forgotten. Pocahontas, *he* sent *his* love, and *he* sent us a basket of birds. After this they went into the quick manner, and the meeting came up to the highest pitch of excitement and interest. But while it yet waxing warmer and louder, elder William saw the propriety of restoring order and quiet; and, for this purpose whispered to elder brother R. H., who immediately says, " The brethren and sisters will take their places, and bring forward their seats. So when all were seated, and a song had been sung, elder William spoke for ten or fifteen minutes.

 He said he rejoiced to see the brethren and sisters, have these beautiful gifts; it was real food to his soul, it was what he *loved.* He hoped we should treasure them up, and make a suitable travel. The Gospel was his only treasure. And he wanted his brethren and sisters, to be assured that if he ever *should* fall, the Gospel would not be to blame. It would not be the fault of the Gospel at all. But it would be because he had drank of that "*pizened*" cup; "The lust of the flesh, the lust of the eye, and the pride of life." He wanted his brethren and sisters, to be particular and remember this, and bear it in mind, that if he ever should fail and become a cast-away, that the Gospel is not at all to blame. But all the reason would be, and must forever be, the lust of the flesh, the lust of the eye, and the pride of life. But he did not see any cause of discouragement, brethren and sisters, and hoped every one would press forward to obtain the prize.

After he was seated a few minutes, and a song had been sung, we all arose and packed away our seats, when David Terry spoke a minute, or so, and dismissed the meeting.

They sometimes have what they call a warring gift. It is when some one, or more of the brethren, or sisters, do not cordially respond to all their silly gifts, or do not render a ready and willing obedience to the elders, or give evidence of a waning faith, or by some obnoxious to the leading influence. In such case, perhaps, as once when I was present at an exhibition of this gift, some of the inspired sisters, Elizabeth Dixon, commenced crying woe! woe! woe! and was soon joined by several others, woe! woe! to them that should leave the way of God, or oppose it. And they accompanied these imprecations with a general concert of groaning, shouting, shaking, stamping, and altogether creating such a tumult as was indeed a caution to the unfaithful. And what made this peculiarly terrible, was, that in pretension, and appearance, it was by a supernatural influence. They would have us to understand that this was brought about by the disgust and indignation of the angelic spirits who were invisibly present in the meeting. Invisible to all except the "Seers." Though one could hardly avoid the conclusion from the appearance, that the authors of this tumult were Bedlamites.

If those "warred" against in this manner, withdraw

from the society, why, the saying was, they could not bear "the testimony," "the testimony was too hot for them." If terrified into obedience, and made an humble confession to the elders, that was the end of the matter. Perhaps I ought to say of the brethren, that they seldom joined in this gift. This curious warfare was generally carried on by the sisters.

These gifts were not always confined to their general religious meetings. The following case occurred in elder William's, or the east family, shortly before I left. Ellen Wier, a young sister, about 16 years of age, became a subject of these warring gifts. She was indentured to elder William, by her parents, and consequently subject to him. She was naturally a sprightly, intelligent, active girl. In the gift of turning, there was no sister who could turn more handsomely, and rapidly, than she. And she had been subject to some "beautiful visions," her visions were sometimes refered to by the Shakers as wonderful.

But at this age she had become dissatisfied with her condition, and longed for her liberty. And conseqnently did not render that reverence and humiliating obedience to her superiors which she had formerly. In consequence of this, she was subjected to various penances and humiliations, such as being compelled not only to kneel, but also to prostrate herself before sister Nancy, or the second eldress, putting her face to the floor. But without effect. She continued rebellious; and hence, the warring gifts. One Sabbath, while in her room, the inspired ones made a bold attack upon her. After making a terrible tumult, and bearing a hot testimony against "the world, flesh, and the devil," they addressed her as follows: pretending to be under a spiritual influence, and assuming the language of the Almighty in the great sentence of the last judgment, they said to her with a terrible manner, "Depart ye cursed into everlasting fire." "You are not worthy to be with the people of God, and we don't want you here. Depart, the quicker the better." The leaders in this affray, were Sarah Smith, who had the care of Ellen, Mary Ann Wollison, and Elizabeth Dixon. They were joined by others.

The poor girl suffered a great deal from such treatment. But since we left, I hear she has obtained her freedom. The principal prophets, and prophetesses, not unfrequently leave them, and deny the reality of all their visions, and revelations. They tell us plainly, that they make these pretensions to please the elders. The elders having once sanctioned their revelations, still maintain that they were really inspired; but having become corrupted through the lust of the flesh, are now blinded, and deny the truth. But we should say, that, while they are connected with the Shakers they are interested witnesses. It being important to their union and good standing to seem to be inspired. Besides, in the excitement of a Shaker meeting, they may think themselves inspired when they are not. They may, therefore, be deceivers, or deceived themselves. And, therefore their testimony cannot be depended upon. But in the latter case, when they have withdrawn from that people, they have no motive to deceive at all. And in their sober second consideration of the matter they are not likely to be deceived themselves. Therefore their testimony is good. And they were never inspired by any spirit but that of the natural body. It was their own deceived imagination, or their own invention. It is not improbable that animal magnetism has in many cases something to do with it.

But as long as the brethren and sisters, can be made to believe these things, they have their effect. And they do believe; a majority of the members of the Shaker community, I have no doubt, most seriously and devoutly believe that all which professes to be revelation, and is sanctioned by the elders, is really such. And every time they see any of these manifestations of whirling, jerking, shaking, twisting, winking, &c., it begets in them a degree of awe and religious fear. And something of this takes place at almost every meeting. And they meet to worship about five times a week. By this means, they are brought into the most perfect submission to their Lead; the elders and ministry. It is the worst kind of slavery. The mind is enslaved by means of this superstition.

I will here notice some of their greatest efforts to impress the less credulous. In such important gifts, the instruments to administer them, are specially appointed by the ministry. And they are careful to appoint those who are most competent to perform in the case. The following gift, if it is not true, must be regarded as very blasphemous. I saw no evidence of its reality, and the predictions which accompanied it, have already been falsified. The Gift is denominated,

"The Gift of Holy Mother Wisdom."

This gift was administered to the people, the Shakers, in the spring of 1843, previous their mountain meeting in the month of May ; previous to my coming among them. Before going upon the mountain in 1844, it was thought best by the ministry, that those who had come among them since it was administered, should also receive it. Accordingly elder William opened the subject to me, and eldress Catherine to the sisters.

Now all such extraordinary occasions as the administration of an important gift, or attending meeting on the " Holy mount" as it is called, is an occasion for a call upon all the brethren and sisters for a confession of all sins, which have not been confessed. During my conference with elder William on this occasion, he opened to me with much solemnity the subject of this gift.

He said this doctrine of the existence of both male and female in the Godhead, had of late received much attention : and was " a growing thing in the world." He solemnly assured me that in receiving this gift, I should realize the presence of a superior power. That to those who had received it, it was very piercing. Searching out the deepest thoughts of their inmost souls. In a word that it was an immediate and special manifestation of God.

Those of us who were to receive it were assembled in the meeting room, dressed in our Sunday clothes. The ministry, and the instruments, and the elders of our family were already there, and had taken their positions. The instruments were Martha Van Valin, and Judith Collins, the chief prophetesses in society. They belonged to the church order. They were seated together, near the center of the room, with their backs towards the eastern wall. The ministry and elders were standing behind them.

After some explanatory remarks, by Br. Grove, of the ministry, assisted by sister Dana, also of the ministry, the ceremony proceeded. First with some little boys from the West family who had not yet received the gift. Next with the sisters, two at a time. As I was the only brother to receive the gift, elder William very kindly accompanied me in the gift, lest as I suppose, I should be embarrassed in receiving it alone. The ceremony was merely repeated to each party of us, and was as follows. I have already described the position of the instruments and elders.

Martha was first seized apparently with an irregular and involuntary nodding, or jerking of the head, and waving of the right hand in all directions; or, as they term it she was taken under operations. This is their sign, and evidence of inspiration. It is believed they are possessed of some heavenly spirit. After a few moments of such operations, she puts the following question, (to the elders if the subject be a brother, and to the eldress if a sister) " Elder William, do you consider this brother a good believer?" The elder replies, " yea, I consider that brother David has good faith, understanding faith; and is endeavoring to live up to it."

This answer seemed to satisfy *"holy mother wisdom ;"* for the great OMNISCIENT, who it was pretended was incarnated in Martha Van Valin at the time, seemed to ask the question for information. It was said to us that she could discern our deepest thoughts. And surely if God were present, he would have no need to ask questions. But the elder being exalted above the deity, could give the desired information. At receiving which " *Holy Mother* " immediately responds " YEA TRULY IT MUST BE SO." But to proceed, after receiving this information, she gave a short exhortation and some intimation of the gift to be bestowed, when the subject makes seven low bows, and repeats after sister Dana or some other one the following words, "Holy, Holy Mother Wisdom! I thank thee for thy great condescension and blessing, and for thy love and mercy to me." Then kneeling down, Holy Mother Wisdom speaking through the instrument says, "*Around thy head I place a golden band. On it is written the name of me, Holy Mother Wisdom! the Great Jehovah! the Eternal God! Touch not mine anointed.*" Then rising up, the subject is required to make seven low bows in thankfulness for the gift. After this I voluntarily remarked, " I trust I am duly thankful for all the gifts which I receive." This voluntary expression, immediately drew from Holy Mother an extemporaneous song, promising me her blessing.

After this the prophetess Judith Collins who sat beside Holy Mother during the ceremony, rose up and began to prophesy; being under operations, and bowing continually and very low. Declaring among other things that brother David should be a preacher of the gospel to God's people, and the world should gather to him to know the way of God. After a little season, Holy Mother proposed to the sisters to ask of her some special gift, promising that whatever they asked should be granted.—Some asked for more faith. Some for more humility &c.

To conclude this religious farce, the ministry assured us that if we continued faithful, the mark which we had received would continue bright to spiritual eyes, and we should be known by it in the eternal world. They charged us solemnly, never from any consideration to speak of this gift to unbelievers. And if we ever spoke of it among ourselves it must be in a very solemn manner.

Some will consider this gift not only as a solemn mockery but as really blasphemous, and will perhaps feel to blame me for the part I acted. I can only make this apology. I knew not beforehand what the gift was to be. The intimations of the elder were very indefinite and vague. I could not know beforehand and until I had examined them, but their pretensions to inspirations and revelations were good and true. If they were good and true, then I had an unbounded interest in them. If they were false, I should be the better able to bear my testimony against them, when I had proved them to be so. This book is that testimony. I believe I took the only method of ascertaining what Shakerism is. I was never active in any of their gifts, but merely passive. I never pretended to believe in their gifts. I merely submitted to them silently and passively. Being exhorted by the elders not to oppose them if I did not believe in them. They assured me that " these little simple gifts could not hurt any body." Some would think I should have borne my testimony against them on the spot. But I did not think it wise or expedient. Had I borne my testimony against the first gifts I witnessed, I should have not been permitted to witness any more. Some will think it unnecessary that I should remain among them so long as two years. But I learned more of the mysteries of Shakerism during the last six months, than all the rest of the time I was among them. It may be thought silly that I should have faith enough in Shakerism even, to make an examination of it. But I say in answer to this, their pretensions are little more absurd or ridiculous, than the pretensions of other denominations to *their* peculiar doctrines and practices. I plainly told the elders that I did not and could not believe these things without evidence. I knew not but they might be true, I was open to conviction.

The reader will be inclined to ask if the Shakers themselves believe these gifts. A large portion of the common members most sincerely and devoutly believe all the elders tell them is true ; and are filled with awe and amazement whenever there is any manifestation of these gifts. But ask them why they believe in these things, and their only answer is, " I feel that it is a reality." But what evidence is there that there is any reality in these things. " I feel that it is a reality. I know it is true." This is the beginning and ending of the discussion with them. Though the elders quote much scripture, and explain it in their own way. The swift turning is sometimes offered as evidence of divine assistance: but the more intelligent know very well that all this can be done by practice, and therefore is no evidence of divine assistance. The "gifted ones" pretend to tell the thoughts and feelings of the brethren and sisters. But in telling these things, they only tell them what they have already confessed to their elders. But the simple ones cannot conceive how the prophets should know these things which they have only confessed to their elders; and the elders are pledged to keep them secret. But I will treat these things in another place. Suffice it for the present to say, there is no evidence of the reality of their gifts; unless we reckon the contortions of body and face and limb which accompany them. And these anybody can practice who chooses to make himself so ridiculous.

I must now proceed to another great and important gift, which followed the last, and seemed to be its counterpart. These two gifts were said to be the greatest notice of God to man ever known. As the first was from "Holy Mother Wisdom," so the last was termed,

The gift of the Father and the Son.

It was administered in June 1844. These gifts I believe were administered to all the families in the denomination. In this gift, God the Father and his Son Jesus Christ incarnate themselves, each in a different individual (a brother) and manifest themselves through them to the people. The instruments through whom the gift is administered to each society, are appointed by the ministry of that society. And the selection is made from the members of the same society. So God and Christ have recently manifested themselves through as many different individuals as there are societies of Shakers in the world. The instruments selected in the society where we were, for this purpose were Joseph Wicker and Simon Maybee of the Church family. Joseph is second elder in the Church family or order. Simon Maybee is one of its deacons. I believe I have before given some intimation of the character of Joseph, nevertheless I will here repeat what I wrote down at the time this gift was administered.

Joseph is a man possessing more than ordinary abilities,

and has acquired an education superior to that of any other person in the village. He was the principal teacher of their school for a number of years. And ever since has had possession of the books, indeed, of all the science and literature in the society. He is cunning, observing, and has a tolerable knowledge of human nature. Is a man of rather dignified appearance; and is said to be "the most inspired of any one in the society." In a word, he is THE prophet of the society. In this gift, it is believed that God the Father, took possession of his body, and through him personally communicated with the members of this society.

Simon Maybee is a man of ordinary abilities and ordinary education. He was appointed by the ministry as the instrument through whom the Son of God appeared and manifested himself to the inhabitants of the " city of peace." He spoke to us as though he was Jesus Christ himself.

About a week previous to the administration of this gift a revelation was read to us by elder William at our evening meeting, announcing the coming of the promised gift, and prescribing our conduct in the mean time. The most important of the directions were, that we should kneel every time we assembled for worship. Should sing no worded songs. That is, sing simply the tunes without words. Using instead of words something like the following; lo lo lo liddle diddle dum, te hoot te hoot te diddle te hoot &c. Such are called noted songs in distinction from worded songs. We should labor in none but slow and solemn manners. That is, should not dance in their meeting, but only march. At our morning and evening meals severally should kneel for the space of five minutes. A few days previous to the administrution of the gift also, we were called upon severally to go before the elders and confess all our sins. This is always done before every such important occasion.

The day and the hour having arrived, all the brethren and sisters were marshalled for the reception of the great gift. The brethren were all assembled in one of the chambers in which we held our union meetings. The elders came in and arranged us in the following order. The older brethren were formed in one rank, and the younger in another, and those composing each rank were also disposed according to their several ages; the older at the head of his rank and the younger at the foot. The two ranks faced inward and were perhaps six or eight feet apart. We were then required to remain in silence until the Lord and Saviour came in. And if it were necessary for us to speak at all to each other, we must speak in a whisper. And when the great Jehovah and his Son entered the room, we were required to rise and make seven low bows and be seated again. What a reception we gave the Deity!! The arrangement of the sisters and the other parts of the house, and their instructions as I learned afterwards, were very similar to ours. We sat in this position for about an hour. During this time the Father and Son arrived under the protection and guidance of the ministry and administered the gift to the elders in their room, and to the eldresses in theirs.

At length, after this tedious and silent waiting, we heard a movement in the hall, a stepping, and the door opened and Jehovah appeared in the person of Joseph Wicker.— Immediately behind him his Son Jesus Christ, in the person of Simon Maybee. Followed by the ministry, and the elders of our family. The Father *alias* Jo. Wicker was under " operations;" his head rolling from side to side, his eyes winking and blinking, his body reeling and jerking, and his lips moving and whispering. The operations of the Son were different, merely jerking the body occasionally from side to side. We rose simultaneously on their entrance and performed our bowing according to order. When the Lord passed along under operations, in front of one rank of the brethren, and back in front of the other, stopping a little in front of every brother, whispering to himself as though reading his heart.

Having passed round in this manner, he drew himself up into a position to address us, became composed and dignified, and addressed us something after the following manner.

"I the Lord God who in former times communed with my servant Job, and with Moses, brought my people out of Egypt through the red sea, and manifested myself to them from Mt. Sinai, and at various other times and manners, am pleased also in these latter days, to manifest myself in love and mercy to you the people of my choice, and bestow on you my gracious blessing."

Having addressed us thus collectively for about three minutes, he was again taken under operations, and passed up to the head of the aged brethren's row, and began by making a personal address to aged Philip :—Now Philip was above ninety years old and very deaf; so that the Lord was obliged to speak to him in a much louder voice than to the rest. The address was one of sympathy in the trials and afflictions which he had endured, telling him that he (the Lord) had permitted these things for his good, and assured him of his continued protection and blessing, encouraging him to be faithful unto the end &c. And concluded by enumerating some of the principal of his virtuous acts, and saying, "FOR THESE THINGS I CROWN THEE WITH THE SEAL OF MY APPROBATION." At the same time gently touching his head with the fore finnger of his right hand.

And then turning to the next brother, addressed him, and also each of the others in a similar manner, closing his address to every one by crowning him with the seal of his approbation.

When the Lord had concluded his speeches to every individual in the room, it became the Son's turn, who in the person of Simon Maybee, arose and giving a few sudden jerks of the body sidewise, right and left, walked up between the two ranks of the brethren with a pompous and swelling air, and attempted a speech which seemed a failure. Turned about and walked back again, having merely represented himself as the Son of God who died to save sinners, and bestowed on us his love and blessing.

The Father, alias Jo Wicker then announced the "patriarch" Job and the prophet Elijah as present, and that they desired us to receive their love and blessing. Sister

Dana said, "The ministry freely unite theirs with it."— That is, they united their love and blessing with that of Job and Elijah. And we all bowed in thankfulness for these great blessings.

The ministry then strictly charged us concerning this great gift of the Father and the Son. That we must have no discussion about it. Must not speak of it lightly ; but if we spoke of it at all, it must be in a very solemn manner. *And on no account whatever*, must we speak of it to an unbeliever. They ordered us to remain in our seats, sitting in silence until the gift was through with in the other parts of the house, and then retired to administer it to the sisters and children. But we brethren presumed to disobey the order this time, and silently withdrew, and went to the shops and other outbuildings, for it being a hot day we were much fatigued with the confinement.

The gift was administered to the sisters and children in a very similar manner as to the brethren. It was a lengthy and tedious affair, continuing from eight or half past eight o'clock in the morning until two in the afternoon. And all the adults in the family male and female were required to remain sitting in silence the whole time ; not leaving our seats without some urgent call. But we brethren having received the gift before the sisters, deserted our post some hours before the time had expired.

It was instructive to observe the effect of these addresses of the Lord upon the individual subjects of them. Some were affected to tears, others were filled with awe and amazement, verily believing it was God who addressed them. Others again seemed indifferent, probably having no faith in the matter. And aged Philip being deaf, did not hear a word that was spoken to him on the occasion, notwithstanding the Lord bending over him spoke louder to him than to the others. Benj. Collins, an aged brother went immediately after the gift to congratulate with Philip on so important a notice from heaven ; he assured me that Philip did not hear a word that was spoken to him, or know who addressed him. Now if it was the Lord who spoke as pretended, his words returned to him void of effect. He evidently intended to make Philip hear, but did not succeed. He evidently thought Philip heard or he would have spoken louder. Now who can believe that the Lord could be so deceived and disappointed? Who can believe that the Lord would come down from heaven and incarnate himself in a human being, make a formal address to an old man and not make him hear it! This little incident is sufficient of itself to prove the whole a deception; a game played upon the ignorant to keep them in subjection. It was not the Lord who spoke to us, but Jo Wicker.

It was wonderful to the brethren and sisters how he could tell them so many of their thoughts and feelings, and even intimate to them their profound secrets, unless indeed he was the great discerner of our thoughts. But this was no riddle to me. They (the brethren and sisters) had already faithfully disclosed all these things to the elders. It is a part of their religion to have no secrets of their own independent of the elders; all are faithfully divulged. All sins are confessed. A day is appointed, but a very short time previous to this gift, on which every one must come before the elders for this purpose. The brethren and sisters do not seem to be aware that every thing of importance which they open to the elders is faithfully carried to the ministry, and that the ministry would therefore be able to inspire the prophet with all the facts he might need. The elders always have a meeting at the ministry's shop directly after a day of confession; although they are pledged to the brethren and sisters not to divulge their confessions. This is a part of the game.

The address of Joseph, (or the Lord) to me in the gift of the Father was general in its character. Commended me for having come among the true people; said I had a vehement spirit against evil; sympathised with me in my past afflictions and disappointments; especially in my having believed that I had many times attained almost to a position in life which would yield permanent happiness, but had been unexpectedly cut off from it; alluding doubtless to the Hopedale affair as one particular. He (the Lord) had witnessed all this and even had a hand in it for my good; and says, "I will try you yet farther." But for my faithfulness to his light and influence, for my *honesty* in all things, he was graciously pleased to *Crown me with the seal of his approbation.*

What will the Shaker elders say to this? I hear that since I have left them, they accuse me of having been a hypocrite. But here in this great gift, sanctioned by all the lead, and pronounced by them as the greatest notice of heaven ever received by mortals, even in this gift their Jehovah pronounced me *honest* and as *having lived up to his light and influence And crowned me with the seal of his approbation.* What more could the Lord have said to the most perfect? And will they presume to condenm those whom the Lord approves? This rather goes to show that the elders themselves do not believe in the reality of the gift. I am fully persuaded that they do not believe in the pretended revelations of their prophets and prophetesses. But the gift is for the common members; if they believe it, it answers its end. The ministry observed afterwards, that the gift had this good effect; "to make the brethren more constant in their confessions, more faithful in obedience to their Lead." This is the great aim of the Lead in all their management.

The reader will be inclined to ask how I could tolerate so much blasphemy. I answer. I could not know beforehand what the gift would be. And I desired to know what the Shakers would do. I did not think it a suitable time and place to testify against it on the moment. But immedaitely after receiving this gift, my wife and myself resolved not to unite with any more Shaker gifts until we knew what they were. This therefore was the last great gift administered while we were among them. I will speak of some gifts which took place previous to this, and perhaps not quite so presumptuous, but equally showing the character of their pretended revelations.

Since writing the above account of the gift of the Father and Son, I have received from a correspondent who still dwells among the people, information that at New

The gift of the Father and Son.

Lebanon (the head of influence) the members prostrated themselves with their faces to the floor while the gift was administered. The elders and minister standing. The instruments who administered the gift at N. L. were three instead of two, viz. the Father, Son, and a holy Angel or Spirit. The part of the two last mentioned persons was to warn the brethren and sisters of the awful consequences of leaving the "way of God."

I do not exactly understand who was designed to be represented by the "holy angel," but as the Shakers are not trinitarians, probably the Holy Ghost was not intended. They believe the Holy Ghost to be of the feminine gender, and the same was represented in the gift of "holy Mother Wisdom," by a female. This "holy angel" was represented by one of the brethren.

I say *represented*, but it was pretended and believed that the instruments were the real incarnation of the persons they represented.

There is no doubt of the correctness of these statements.

The Cleansing Gift.

In this gift a day is devoted specially to cleansing the out-buildings and the yards about the buildings. This revelation came in 1843. And by it, the 23d of Sept. in every year for ten years is set apart for this purpose. This special revelation and command was received at New Lebanon, through the prophet Philemon Stewart, to this effect. A little book containing the revelation is read in the several families throughout the denomination, on the evening previous to the day for cleansing. The requirement is, that on the morning of that day, we rise at four o'clock; which is a half hour earlier than usual. At half past four the family must assemble in the meeting room of their dwelling. It is required of every one to make a low bow as he or she enters the room. (But the bowing was dispensed with in 1844.) After taking their places in the meeting room, they must sing the following song,—entitled the *Voice of God*. The following are the words.

"I will roar, roar, roar, yea I will howl, howl, howl in my fury saith the Lord, because of the abominations that rest in my Zion. And I will send forth a curse, curse, curse, yea I will send forth a heavy curse upon the inhabtants that dwell in her."

Then all kneel down in prayer, and while on our knees, bow three times. We are to eat no meat on that day, but live "light;" for our supper we are to have nothing but bread and water. A band of singers shall be selected from among the brethren, by the elders, and shall march with the elders in solemn procession through every room in all the brethren's workshops, and other out-buildings, repeatedly singing as they pass along through every room and building, the song quoted above. It is said they shall sing it "with shame and confusion." And every time they sing the words, "And I will send forth a curse, curse, curse," the elders shall stamp their feet with indignation. And when they come to any place where they believe any filthiness has been committed, they shall shake. If the sin has been confessed, they shall kneel down and pray that they may be forgiven. These are the exercises of the forenoon. In the afternoon, commencing at one o'clock, they are to march through all the fields in the same manner, repeating the same song and ceremonies.

A band of singers is also chosen from among the sisters, who march with the eldresses in solemn procession, in the forenoon through all the sister's workshops, nurse rooms, the laundry, &c. with the same ceremonies, singing repeatedly the above song, shaking and stamping as they go. In the afternoon they pass through the yards, and about the building repeating the same ceremonies. In the evening, after our supper of bread and water, the dwellng house is gone over with in the same manner as the shops and fields are in the day time. With this exception however; instead of the above song the following is sung.

It is entitled, " *cleanse your sanctuary.*" The following are the words.

" Purify your hearts O my children, cleanse your sanctuary clean, clean your dwellings and prepare for holy Mother to meet with you."

The eldresses and singing sisters go through all the rooms occupied by the sisters, singing as they go. The elders and singing brethren through those occupied by the brethren, singing as they go. The rest of the brethren and sisters must be in their several rooms during this performance. Thus ends the day. The employment of all the brethren and sisters, save the elders and singers, is, cleansing every dirty or filthy place on the premises, mending broken windows, putting things in place, &c. No other work is to be done during the day, and no songs are to be sung but those quoted above or others that are like it.

This day's performance is exceedingly silly and ridiculous. The most devout Shakers even are ashamed of it. They dread exceedingly any visiters from the world on that day. For the command is unanimously acknowledged to be from heaven, and therefore they must " Roar " and "Howl" in the song, about all the buildings and fields, let who will be present.

A Revelation concerning the Personality of the Devil.

There had been some discussion among some of the brethren, on the subject of the personality of the devil. Those who denied this personality, were reproved by the ministry for holding a false doctrine. Some information seemed to be needed on this point. Accordingly the prophet at the head of influence, Philemon Stewart, was directed by the ministry to labor for a revelation on the subject. He brought forth one which our ministry read to us on their next visit to our family. I recorded immediately after hearing it read, what I could remember. It professed to be a proclamation by God, of his character and attributes, and closed by teaching us the origin of evil. In this revelation, God proclaimed himself as the ETERNAL TWO; the Father and Holy Mother Wisdom. The male and female blended or united in one, Co-equal and Co-existent, by whom the universe and all it contains (except evil) was produced. In this revelation, God absolutely denies all participation in the production of evil, either actively or by assent. But he assures us that the two principles *good* and *evil* are self-existent and eternal. The good principle is God. He created the heavens and the earth, men and angels. Then the evil principle which is called Apolyon, signifying Destroyer, beheld the glory of God's creation and was filled with envy. And now for the first time made his appearance in opposition to God, having come to destroy his creation. Then Lucifer, who was an angel of God, deserted, and together with the angels which adhered to him, went over to Apolyon. This is the war spoken of in the ancient Scriptures. Michael and his angels fought and the devil and his angels. The devil which is Apolyon would have destroyed the work of God, but God prevailed over him and set bounds to his influence, and shut him up with all his legions in the regions of darkness. It was this Apolyon tempted Mother

Eve in the garden, having appeared to her in the form of a serpent. Her sin was the indulgence of the flesh for her own gratification, and not for the propagation of the species, nor in union with the will of God.

Elder Nathaniel Demming, who was the head of our ministry, made remarks concerning Apolyon. That he was still exerting himself to destroy the work of God, by tempting men to sin, and especially to an excessive indulgence of the flesh. But he is limited by the power of God. He also spoke of the blight on potatoes as an evidence that the predictions of their prophets were about to be fulfilled. They had predicted that there was to be a grievous famine in the land. And that 1843 was to be last fruitful season. He says, " Every body thought that the potato crop could not fail." It would seem that God has begun with the potatoes, to show to mankind how utterly futile are all their hopes. It was rumored among us, and probably was true, that the society at New Lebanon had prepared a store house, and had commenced filling it, in preparation for the famine. It was " spoken," that is prophesyed for the comfort of the Shakers, that the food of the faithful and obedient, though reduced to the very smallest allowance, should satisfy them.

After the reading of the roll, and the remarks of the elder, I asked the privilege of putting a question to him for information; thinking also that it might be interesting to the brethren and sisters to know his opinion on the subject. Elder Nathaniel said, perhaps it would not be a proper question to ask *there*; but I could not be the judge of that myself. Thinking there was no impropriety in the question, I proposed it thus. " Are we to regard the blight upon the potatoes as a direct providence of God, as a punishment of sin? And are we to regard God as the punisher of sin?" Elder Nathaniel hesitated. And the rest of the ministry with the elders of our family, immediately joined in saying that elder Nathaniel was deaf, and could not understand the question, and that I had better propose it at another time.

After this meeting was closed, I was honored with an

interview with the " blessed ministry " and elders, in the elders' room ; and was permitted to renew my question. The minister gave his decision in the affirmative.

I then said to him that it occured to me that if the GOOD PRINCIPLE was male and female, and had produced a creation, the same might also be the case with the EVIL PRINCIPLE ; and that this male and female principle may have produced a world of intelligences. The ministry smiled, and said, they had thought it might be so, and that the world was full of evil spirits, the production of the evil principle.

This brings to our view, a new and important doctrine, to distinguish this already very peculiar people from all other religious people in the world. They have laid a new foundation for their religion. It is neither the *trinity*, nor the *unity*, but a DUALTY of the Godhead. *The Father* and *Holy Mother Wisdom.* These first parents of creation, have also a SON and a DAUGHTER ; JESUS CHRIST and MOTHER ANN LEE. These last are the parents of the new, the spiritual creation. And they are often refered to as their heavenly parents. So they hold not only to the doctrine of the two original and opposite principles of good and evil from which all things have sprung, but they also dualise the good principle, and make it the author of a creation after its own kind and sex. They likewise dualize the evil principle and make it the author of a creation after its own kind and sex.

The Annual Fast.

The proclamation for this fast was given in 1842 and is read and observed yearly. Having heard it read on the night preceding the 22d Dec. 1844, the day on which it was observed, I wrote down what I could remember of the proclamation, and its observance.

First is an address of father William to the Instrument. (Father William, is William Lee, brother to Mother Ann Lee; and acted with her during her reign, and for this reason is called father.) His address is a sort of charge in which the Instrument (probably Philemon Stewart) is addressed as the annointed instrument of God ; said to be annointed by his holy power and wisdom.

The Instrument then receives the proclamation directly from a holy angel sent forth from God's eternal throne of light and power; and is charged to allow his hand to be guided by the angel unrestrained.

God proclaims himself as the eternal Judge of all things &c. &c. and declares that he has long beheld the secret sins and abominations of his people, and their endeavors to cover them from his chosen witnesses; (the elders to whom they should have confessed them) and he threatens them with his judgments if they do not honestly and faithfully confess to him before his chosen witnesses every secret sin and abomination, even to the mentioning the time and place of its commission. They shall *humble themselves before his chosen and annointed witnesses and ask their prayers and their blessings.* If they have no particular sins to confess, *then they shall go and hmmble themselves before his chosen witnesses and ask their blessing.* For this purpose the fast is proclaimed and held. On this day we are required to rise at the fourth hour in the morning; go into meeting at the fifth hour, and bow low as we enter the meeting room. We must eat nothing on this day but pure bread; which says God, I have given for the main support of my creature man; and drink nothing but pure water. And also, to all our animals, on this day their food shall be dealt out to them prudently and sparingly. [*Note.* Even the animals of the Shakers having observed a fast, have a better moral character than those of the world.]

We are forbidden to frequent our places of employment on this day, but are required to collect in our dwellings and spend our time in contemplation, repentance and confession. When we kneel down before taking our meals of bread and water on this day, the elder says over the following prayer, and each sentence is repeated after him by the family in concert.

"*Holy holy Mother Wisdom, we partake of this the blessing of our God, in remembrance of thy love and kindness, and in obedience to thy righteous will."* [*Note.* Doubtless the greater part of the brethren and sisters understood this prayer to be offered to Mother Ann Lee. But some understood it to be offered to Holy Mother Wisdom; the feminine person in the Godhead.]

After the morning service, the first elder receives the older brethren into his room one by one to hear their "openings" or confessions. The second elder in another room receives the boys and young men under his care for the same purpose. The same course is pursued by the eldresses with the sisters " on the other side of the house " as they term it.

This duty occupied the greater portion of the day. We are not permitted to "labor," that is to march or dance in our meetings on this day, " but must sound forth in our meetings prayer and praise in solemn songs."

On the following morning we must enter the meeting room again precisely at five o'clock, and every one is required to make a low bow as we enter the room. After singing two songs in praise to God, the meeting closed and thus ended the fast. This fast is not always kept on the same day of the month. But the Lord having given permission to his holy annointed ministry and elders to do with it what their wisdom should dictate, they presume to alter the day if it come on a week day, to the Sabbath. This is done for the purpose doubtless to save time for secular business.

" *A Holy, Sacred and Divine Roll and Book from the Lord God of heaven, to the inhabitants of earth: revealed in the united Society at New Lebanon, county of Columbia, State of New York, United States of America.*"

The above is the title of a book which may properly be called the "The Shaker Bible." The motto is, "Read and understand all ye in mortal clay."

This book is " Received by the Church of this communion, and published in union with the same." "Printed in the united Society, Canterbury, N. H. 1843." The book is in two parts. The first part has been published to the world. The second part is printed only for the use of the Society, and probably never will be published. It was kept back through the influence of the more thoughtful and prudent among them, who had doubts as to its reception and influence upon an intelligent public. Since they have sent forth the First Part, and it has been received according to its merits; producing no impression either good or bad, they will doubtles never receive any command from the Lord to publish the Second part. Though in merit, I regard the second part as much superior to the first. The first part is extremely prosy and tedious reading. It is composed by one author, who is evidently of medium talent, without much education or knowledge of human nature. And withal very ignorant of the intelectual and literary condition of the world at large. This last remark is applicable to the Shaker ministry generally, or they would never have attempted to impose such trash upon the world as a revelation from God. The second part was composed in the following manner. After the first part had been printed and read throughout the denomination, all the members who were competent were required to write a testimony concerning it. All these testimonials were collected by the ministry, and out of the mass selections were made and compiled for the second part. Some of these exhibit strong and brilliant imaginations, and no small share of natural talent. Having been permitted to read this second part, I took the liberty privately to make such extracts from it as I thought would show the character of the work and be interesting to the reader. These will be introduced and noticed in their proper place.

I will here give a more particular notice of the first part, of which I have an entire copy. One object of the Shakers in publishing this work was doubtless, to silence the oft repeated inquiry put to them by the world; "If you have the true gospel, why not preach it to the world? why is your religion so private and exclusive?" They consider that they have now by this book, given to the world the true gospel. They were required by a special revelation to make the following distribution of the book to the world, as nearly as I can recollect. A copy to the

President, and one to the Vice President of the United States; a copy to the Governor of every State in the United States; a copy to each of the Sovereigns of Europe, and one to the head of every other known power in the world.

It is worthy of notice here that although the Shakers profess to speak in their inspirations all the languages that were ever spoken on the earth, yet in sending out their gospel to the world, it was given to all the different nations in our own language. Except as the English is here and there interspersed with what is called "unknown" language. And indeed it is unknown; for I presume no linguist on earth could find any meaning to it. Their unknown languages, which are spoken at their meetings generally, by their inspired ones, are indeed *Unknown;* not being known even to the speaker of them. They are the veriest gibberish which has no meaning; as the specimens which I have given in their songs and shall give from the book. The gospel of Jesus Christ when preached by the apostles at Jerusalem, was heard by those assembled there from the nations round about in their own several languages; and not like the Shakers "Unknown," which is unknown to every body. So also the gospel of Jesus Christ was "preached to the poor;" but this Shaker gospel is given to the rich, and the honorable of this world. " Not many mighty, not many honorable according to this world, were called by the gospel of Christ." But this Shaker gospel is given to such exclusively; to the kings and governors of this world. I could not obtain a copy on any condition to bring away with me. I think the elders were permitted by special privilege to give out a few copies of the first part among such clergymen in the world as they believed would profit by it. I obtained a copy which had been given to a clergyman.

This work after the title page, commences thus.

"*A proclamation of the Lord God of heaven and earth, sent forth by his blessed Son, and revealed in flames of fire upon his holy mountain, for mortal hand to write.*"

The above is followed by an "Introduction to the proclamation." And this *introduction* is signed by Philemon Stewart, the writer of the book. In this introduction the writer tells how he was called upon by the holy angel to go up into the holy mountain and prepare to write the communication from heaven. " The holy mount " spoken of is a place where they hold occasional meetings in the open air. It is a small mountain near their village, spoken of in another place.

After the introduction, and preceding the proclamation is the following.

" The word of God, to his holy Son Jesus Christ the Savior of men."

" Take this short roll of my word, go forth to earth, and read aloud, upon the top of my holy mountain, that one of my servants may understand and correctly write the same.

To this place, I will cause one of my holy angels, who shall bear thee company, to lead the one I have chosen, even in the first watch of the rising sun, to the sacred spot of ground, whereon I will cause my word to be revealed in flames of burning fire."

This is followed by the proclamation itself; which begins thus. " Bow down your heads, all ye who dwell in Zion, and humble yourselves to the dust before me, O ye worms of mortal clay! All flesh shall wither at my presence, and the deceitful worker in Zion shall be consumed by the fire of my burning." Zion here denotes the Shaker community. This proclamation covers about three pages of the book, and is a sort of prelude to the Sacred Roll and Book. It was posted near their meeting house in New Lebanon for a considerable length of time.

The proclamation is followed by " THE WORD OF THE LORD GOD OF HEAVEN To one of his holy and mighty angels of Light, Power, and Truth, as He was about to send him with a Sacred and Solemn Roll of his Word, in mercy to the inhabitants of a perishing earth, and languishing world."

This word to the angel commences thus, " Draw near before my throne, O ye mighty and holy Angels, and all ye Seraphs, spread your wings and lie low in breathless silence, while I sound forth my word and will to this Holy Angel, whom I have commissioned to take this Roll, which I have written with my own hand, and place it safely upon the central dwelling, in the heart of my Zion on earth; and there it shall remain, until the time shall come, that I in my own wisdom, shall send him forth to read the same for mortal hand to write."

I cannot forbear one or two remarks before making further quotations. 1st. The writer of this new revelation, like the author of the book of Mormon and other imposters, imitates the style and expression of the old Testament; and makes God speak bad English, whereas, we should suppose he would be equal in language to the best *modern* grammarian. But this ancient manner of expression has a peculiar charm for the superstitious. He makes God speak of "The first watch of the rising sun." What does this mean? Is the day, as well as the night, divided into watches? Who observes such a division of the day? It is manifest that the writer has gone beyond his inspiration here. It must seem nonsense to himself, when he comes to reflect upon it. I think this manner of the division of time was never applied to the day even by the Jews. The night was appropriately divided by them into watches. They had four watches of the night; the first was from six o'clock in the evening until nine, the second from nine to twelve, the third from twelve to three, and the fourth from three to six in the morning. But this "watch of the rising sun," is a new revelation, not of God but of Philemon Stewart.

This new revelation, The Sacred Roll and Book, it would seem God sent not in the form of a modern book, or it could not with any propriety be called a *Roll*. Before the invention of paper making, the ancients wrote upon the skins of animals or parchment, joined together by some adhesive preparation or sewing, so as to extend their length indefinitely, or according to the magnitude of the writing; and for convenience were rolled up, or unrolled. But since the invention of paper making, the 'Roll' has been superceded by the far more convenient form of books. The Shakers in their visions see a great many "Rolls." But who can believe that God and the spirits still adhere to this ancient and inconvenient mode of making their written communications? But in the quotation we have made, God is made to say, "This Roll, which I have written with my own hand." If he wrote it, he knows why he wrote it in the form of a Roll. But did he write it? that is the question. And are we required to believe without evidence? During the two years I was with the Shakers, they were continually pretending to be inspired. But I say in all sincerity, that in all their manifestations, I never saw any proof of real inspiration.

This address of God to the angels, occupies about two and a half pages; and then follows, "THE WORD OF THE HOLY AND MIGHTY ANGEL, to the inspired writer, who had been at the angel's service, previous to the writing of this Roll, in showing forth signs, both strange and in a manner unaccounted for by mortals; yet evidently showing that heavy tribulation for the people of God, was even at their doors."

This address occupies about two pages of the work. I will quote from it only a single paragraph. The angel says to the writer, "Six hours in each day, I will distinctly read from the Roll for thy mortal hand to write; the words thou shalt clearly understand, as I sound them forth to thee; but the rest part of the day, and time, thou shalt labor under severe distress of soul, and great anguish of spirit."

This quotation shows the manner in which the word was communicated to the writer. It was read in a loud and distinct voice by the angel, from a Roll which had previously been written by the finger of God. It is a "plenary inspiration." Not only is the sentiment inspired, but also the word, letter and punctuation. The writer being asked by some of his brethren if the Roll was actually read to him in a loud voice, replied, that "the voice sounded as loud as thunder." There is much said about the sufferings of the writer to prepare him for the task.

His great anguish of soul and spirit. I am unable to see why God should inflict such distresses upon his chosen instrument; or why pain should qualify him for the work. It is clear that it is a desideratum with the writer to make a display and produce an impression. To this end all the solemn addresses which we have noticed; some by Jehovah, some by angels, and one by the writer; add to these the distresses of the writer; no doubt indicated by dreadful writhings of body and contortions of countenance; and it appears very terrible to the true believer.

The next subject in order in this book is the "INTRODUCTION TO THE SACRED ROLL, BY THE HOLY ANGEL." It occupies a little more than one page. It commences with a most solemn charge to the reader as to the manner of reading the book; and closes thus; " Therefore prepare, make no delay. And I solemnly warn you (says the angel,) make not this book a subject of speculation, for money's sake; for God forbiddeth that his sacred givings should be so used by mortals.

" Ministers professing to preach the pure gospel of Christ, are required, by the spirit of God, as soon as they can obtain a copy, to keep one sacred in the pulpit of their house of worship, as directed in the latter part of this book, and to be used accordingly."

Boards of foreign missions are also required, by his Holy Spirit, to translate correctly, into other languages, and print copies sufficient to circulate in all foreign nations throughout Christendom, and wherever missions have been extended, making charges for the books sufficient only to remunerate them for their trouble; and this is to be done, if possible, in two years from the commencement of the year eighteen hundred and forty four, as will be seen towards the close of this Roll.

" All printers, who may have a wish to reprint this book, are under the most solemn charge, (as will be seen by reading it through,) not to alter, add, or diminish, a word herein contained. And to make such charges for the books, of those who may wish to purchase, as will justly compensate them for their expense, and no more, saith the holy and mighty angel of God." Dated New Lebanon, Feb. 2, 1843, 12 o'clock. M. This shows the high expectations of the Shakers in relation to this work. They expected it would at once become popular, and the books in so great demand that the worldly minded would make them a source of pecuniary profit. That the clergy would receive them in faith and reverence them. And that they would even supersede the Bible in all missionary enterprises. This was the faith of all true Shakers, as I found by conversing with them. One said he thought it "a little *superior* to the Bible." I was enquired of in one of their union meetings, how soon I thought the world would reprint the "Sacred Roll?" When I suggested that they might never reprint it, one of the elder brethren answered very sharply, that it would be reprinted within a year. And this seemed to be the feeling of all the faithful believers; that the book would be reprinted and widely circulated; and would convert a large portion of the world to Shakerism. And that God would send dreadful judgments upon all who did not receive it and come over and confess their sins to the elders. Some preparations were made to receive the converts to be made by it. I heard many predictions of awful judgments which were to come upon the obstinate and impenitent.

We have now arrived at the main work, which is introduced to the reader by the following heading of the first chapter: "The Sacred, Solemn and Sealed Roll, opened and read by the Mighty Angel."

From this I must quote sparingly and reserve space for quotations from the second part, which is not given to the world, but is far more interesting than the first, which is now under consideration. In this book, as might be expected, God is made to confirm all the peculiar doctrines of Shakerism, and to assert the correctness of all the interpretations of Scripture, which the Shakers have quoted and interpreted to prove those doctrines.

We read on the 30th page, "And, as I have commanded

in the second manifestation of the same spirit, now in this your day, though you believe it not, which is through the Daughter of Zion, constituting a spiritual Mother, the second Anointed One, who now stands in her proper lot and place, with blessed Lord and Savior, at the head of my new and spiritual creation, now established on the earth; and her name is, and forever, shall be, MOTHER ANN LEE."

Now this is a plain declaration: no one can mistake it; he that runs may read. In this the chief corner stone of Shakerism is laid. Who now can mistake or doubt the doctrine? None certainly will dare doubt if he heed the awful judgments pronounced against him. Read the following, quoted from part VI. of the "Roll." "Therefore great must be thy punishment; the cup of trouble and affliction which thou hast filled to others, shall be filled to thee double. The abominations and pollutions with which thou hast covered the earth, shall sink with thee, and thy companions, into the lowest depths of hell. Desolation shall stand in thy gate, and destruction shall stare thee in thy face. The cries and shrieks of the tormented in hell shall be thy continual food; for thou repentest not at my warning, and I no longer hearken to thy cry, saith the Lord. * * * I called in mercy, but thou wouldst not hearken. I sent messengers unto thee, to warn thee of thy danger, but thou didst deride, mock and shamefully entreat them. The time that I did give thee to prepare, in low humility, for my coming, thou didst put far in the future tense. The sun shall be darkened over thy head, and the earth shall roar in convulsions under thy feet; until she shall swallow down, and devour without mercy, many portions of thy wicked and exalted nations. The high and the low, the rich and the poor, shall fall in one common grave of ruin. And upon your fleets at sea will I pour forth my fury, which shall dash them one against another, until they are buried in the bosom of the deep."

Such kind of revelations as the above, have great power over the minds of the brethren and sisters, and are used by the elders and ministry to procure their obedience. All such revelations when approved by the elders, are received by the brethren and sisters without question or criticism. Any doubt of their genuineness is regarded as a sin. And any such doubt expressed to any but the elders, is a very great misdemeanor. But all intelligent people in the world with whom liberty of conscience has been encouraged, will feel under no obligations to receive such pretensions as revelations from God, without *proof* of their genuineness. The first and great direliction from duty, of the multitudes who have withdrawn from the Shakers, has been the questioning of their pretended revelations. These pretended revelations will not bear investigation at all. The proof that they come from God is entirely wanting. And a candid examination of the subject, generally results in the infidelity of him who presumes to do so.

Chapter 5th is about 5 pages of Scripture quotations concerning the coming of Christ. These are chiefly from the canonical books, but a portion from the 2d of Esdras. By making this quotation as "*passages of Scripture,*" the Lord has sanctioned this book (2d of Esdras) as of equal authority with the other books of the Bible.

Chapter 15th is headed, " PASSAGES OF SCRIPTURE, REFERING TO THE SECOND COMING OF CHRIST IN THE FEMALE."

Here we may expect to find it taught very clearly that Ann Lee is Jesus Christ. God himself is made to select the passages, and remark upon them. I will briefly notice a few of these selections. The first quoted is from Gen. v : i. " This is the book of the generations of Adam. In the day that God created man, in the likeness of God made he him. 2. Male and female created he them, and called their name Adam, in the day they were created."

" Sec. 1. Understand the two foregoing passages : If the first Adam, being male and female, was a correct and true figure of him that was to come as the second Adam, which I bear witness is true, saith the angel, the second

Adam must also be male and female, which is the case, and will so remain to the endless ages of eternity."

This is a fair specimen of Shaker interpretation of Scripture, and of Shaker reasoning. It is characteristic also in another respect, viz. what the argument could not effect is attempted to be done by authority. The argument is not new. It was used by the Shakers before this new revelation was printed. But as they could not make the world see any force in the argument, they claim for it the sanction of God. Or rather they make him to assume it as his own. The premises in the argument is assumed, viz. that *Adam was both male and female.* But how do they establish this premises? Here they will say of course, it is established by the authority of God. But before this revelation was made, they pretended to establish it by the following reasoning. Quoting the 27th verse of the 1st Chapter, which says " Male and female created he them." They insist that this has reference only to Adam, because nothing is said of the creation of Eve in this connexion. Her creation being described in the next Chapter. So that Adam is here spoken of as being both male and female in the same person. In the creation of Eve the female was taken from the male.

Now this reasoning is so clearly and manifestly absurd, that it is difficult to make it appear more so. The plain truth in the case is this. Moses mentions the simple fact that God created the first pair male and female. In the image of God created he him; male and female created he THEM." That is, the two. The man and woman. Because Moses describes the manner of Eve's creation in the second Chapter, is no evidence that the simple fact of her creation is not also mentioned in the 27th verse of the first Chapter. The noun *man*, is used not only here but in many other places in the Bible, to denote the human race, including both sexes. That it is so in the present instance, is clear from the fact that it has pronouns to agree with it in the plural number. " God created *them* male and female," " and blessed *them*," " and said unto *them*." Nothing can be clearer. Nothing can be more absurd than this new Shaker idea, that Adam was both male and female. Unless indeed it be the conclusion they draw from this premises, viz. that Christ of whom Adam was a figure, was also male and female. And in his second appearance married a poor blacksmith in England, and had four children by him. If the premisis is sound, the conclusion is correct, notwithstanding its manifest and gross absurdity. But who can believe it? None certainly can believe it on the ground of such reasoning. It must be received, if received at all, on the ground of its having been revealed to the Shakers. But intelligent people will need very strong proof to convince them that God reveals such things any where.

Still the passages we have noticed are as good proof of Shakerism as any to be found. Though the angel *alias* Philemon Stewart, has quoted a large mass in this (15) chapter, to prove that Christ's second advent to earth was in Mother Ann Lee. Some from the canonical books, and some from the 2d of Esdras. The whole of the xlv Ps. is quoted, and the following remarks made upon it. "The forepart of this Ps. speaketh so clearly of Christ, under the character of the king, that it would seem impossible for any to misunderstand it; and from the ninth verse to the end, speaketh so clearly of the Queen, the Daughter of Zion, and of the virgins that follow her, that none, but such as are willfully blind, can pervert its true meaning, saith the Lord."

"Virgin, meaneth that which is pure and undefiled, whether it be male or female; and such are the virgins, her companions, that follow her into the presence of the king."

This is very plain. Christ in his first appearing is the king. And in his second advent is the queen, alias "Mother Ann Lee." And this is the way Shakerism is proved to be true. If this be God's word, it is true. And the ministry and elders assure us it is. And not only so, but all the *obedient* and faithful under them, have given their written testimony also, that the "Sacred Roll" is the word of God. The ministry required, after the

"Roll" had been read among the Shakers, that every one who was competent should give a written testimony concerning it. Now every Shaker is under absolute authority. And every Shaker knew perfectly well that his peace and well-being in the Shaker community, depended upon his giving a testimony in favor of the inspiration of that book. His home and all his substance is there. But he cannot remain there without the union of the ministry and elders; and their union he can have only on condition of implicit obedience, and *apparent* faith at least in their inspiration. Who then cannot see that every one is an interested witness in the case? The ministry and elders are interested to maintain their authority and influence over the members. The members are interested to maintain their union with their " *Lead*," upon which every thing depends. Their home, their all in this life. For if they leave they can carry nothing with them. They must go penniless and naked as it were. They can have no clothing even, except such Shaker habiliaments as the elders are disposed to allow them. Knowing these facts, it did not seem strange to me that the ministry and elders should be able to obtain a very general testimony among the Shakers in favor of the inspiration of the " Roll." Still I *know* many of them have no faith at all in its inspiration.

A few more brief quotations. " Do you seek for that kingdom * * Where souls know, by actual experience of more than sixty years, that they have found the spirit of the Lord's Christ, revealed in a Mother, whose name was Ann Lee?

" For it hath saved them from all sin, and clothed their souls in a garment of true righteousness, and created in their hearts, that love to Mother, their God and Maker, which surpasseth, in a thousand fold ratio all other loves;

" Which has given them strength and power to resign their lives in martyrdom, if called so to do, rather than deny their faith, or the power by which they received this, from, and through the Queen of Zion, who stands as my first and chosen witness in this last dispensation of my goodness to man.

"Do you seek for that kingdom, where the gospel of a Christ and of a Mother reigneth, united in one?

"Were any of you born, and brought forth into a completed state of existence in the world, by a *father*,—or by a *mother?* Or were you only begotten by a *father*, and then, at the proper time and season, brought forth by a *mother?*

"And by whom were you fed with milk, and dandled at the breast, while in your infancy; by the father,—or by the mother?

"By whose caresses, and soothing hand of comfort, were your troubled spirits pacified to rest? was it not the mother's?"

"Now is'nt this a mighty argument? Is'nt it conclusive?—Professedly it comes from Jehovah, and it proves that none have been born spiritually but the disciples of Ann Lee.

Another argument founded upon Rev. 14: 14. "And I looked, and beheld a white cloud, and upon the cloud *one* sat like unto the Son of man, having on his head a golden crown, &c."

"This which my servant John saw, sitting upon the white cloud, was the *likeness* of the Son of man; therefore it could not be his person; but that same spirit which once dwelt in the person of Jesus. And that same spirit, is now upon earth the second time, making an end of sin, and bringing in everlasting righteousness.

"And this spirit did first appear, and take up its abode, in the *female witness* of my last dispensation of grace and goodness, to the lost race of man.

"The fulness of this work, in its completed order, was perfected, in the witness whose name is recorded on my eternal record, saith the Lord, the DAUGHTER of ZION, the BRIDE, the LAMB's WIFE, who once dwelt in the earthly tabernacle of ANN LEE. The second witness, who stood through great sufferings and tribulation, an able helper and supporter, once dwelt in the mortal body of WILLIAM LEE.

"The third, who was a faithful, true and proclaiming

witness of that everlasting gospel, now sent forth to the inhabitants of earth, once dwelt in the mortal body of James Whittaker.

"These were my three first witnesses, in this last dispensation of my goodness to man; and I proclaim them as such, saith the God of heaven, to the four quarters of the earth; and let him that readeth understand."

William Lee, the second witness, was the natural brother of Ann Lee, and cotemporary with her. James Whittaker was also cotemporary with her, came over from England with her, and succeeded her in the pontificate of Shakerdom.

The argument founded upon Rev. 14 : 14, viz. That the one seen by John sitting upon the cloud, could not be the Son of man, because in the likeness of the Son of man. I shall take liberty to notice, notwithstanding it professes to be the argument of God. This argument had been used a long time by the Shakers before its appearance in this revelation, the *Sacred Roll.*

"It could not be the Son of man because it was his likeness." But why not? Does not every man possess his own likeness? Do we ever see a man distinctly, and not at the same time behold his true likeness? Can there possibly be a more correct likeness of a man, than his own proper person?—But probably this which John saw, was not the person or spirit of Jesus, neither of Ann Lee. It was a vision. Not a vision of Ann Lee, but of the Son of man, or of Jesus Christ.

The grossness of this absurdity, and the gross absurdity of all the pretensions of Ann Lee's being the second appearing of Christ, are manifest the moment we consider that Christ is every where spoken of in the masculine gender. Any idea of a Christ in a feminine gender, is ridiculous in the extreme. The construction which the Shakers put upon certain passages of scripture in applying them to Ann Lee, is so manifestly untenable that instead of depending upon the argument, they now assert that it is confirmed by a new revelation from God. All now depends upon the truth of this new revelation. They make

God to come down from heaven and assert the correctness of all their shallow reasonings and false doctrines. If God has done what they pretend he has, then their doctrines and reasonings are true, if not they are false. Those who can receive the *ipsi dixit* of the Shaker priesthood as infallible, can believe it; none others can. For this is the only proof of the thing. The shrewdness with which the ministry and elders conduct the game of Shakerism is good evidence that they do not believe in the pretensions of their prophets and prophetesses. They are entirely subject to the ministry and elders, and if they do not prophesy to suit them, they are treated as mere pretenders. The prophets and the priesthood have a good understanding. Many of the common members understand the game pretty well, but remain quiet and obedient through policy. The more simple of the common members are deceived; are perfectly honest, fully believing all the strange and peculiar things belonging to Shakerism. Both body and mind are perfectly enslaved. They are the life and strength of the denomination. Through them the ministry are enabled to control the unbelieving.

I have perhaps quoted sufficiently from this book to give some idea of its character and pretensions. The writer occasionally puts in a sentence of unknown language. I will give a few examples. In the last part of the book the prophet Isaiah is made to act his part. It commences thus.

"A PROPHESY FROM THE SPIRIT OF THE ANCIENT PROPHET ISAIAH, COMMUNICATED THROUGH HIS ARCHERS. IN SIX PARTS.

What is meant by *Archers* in this place I cannot imagine. There is no clue given to its meaning in the book, except that they are a kind of messenger sent to us with the prophet's predictions. But why they should be called *Archers* I cannot conceive unless it be that they use the cross-bow. Perhaps they kill game for the prophet. My eye falls upon one paragraph however, in the message of the first archer which may give some clue to their office.

" Cry aloud, O ye archers of heaven, and spare not

your voices on earth. Gird yourselves with the strength of the unicorn, and bend ye the bows of destruction, and let fly the arrows of death : but the humble and penitent, shall ye pass lightly over."

The archer among other questions to the shepherds of Israel, puts to them the following. "*O hail le vincet! Hail le vincet!* and where are you?"

In another place the prophet uses the following expression. "For the rolling of the *Ar van se ka lov*, will surely bring it on you."

One of the archers commences his message thus. "*O Ha len hu mer, I se va lo!* O earth, and all who dwell thereon." Now this unknown language gives an air of mystery to the work, which will have no little influence over the superstitious.

Another chapter has the following heading. "THE WORD OF THE HOLY AND MIGHTY ANGEL OF THE LORD, WHO HATH READ THE SACRED ROLL, AND THAT CONTAINED IN THIS BOOK, FOR MORTAL HAND TO WRITE."

In this the angel gives his name and the names of three others.

"My name, saith the mighty angel of light, power and truth, I will now make known unto you, in my own language; also the names of the other three in their own languages."

"My name says the angel whose quarter is eastward, and stands as first, is HOLY ASSIN DE LA JAH. The second, whose part is second, and quarter westward, is MICHAEL VAN CE VA NE. THE third, whose part is third, and quarter northward, is GA BRY VEN DO VAS TER REEN. The fourth, whose part is fourth, and quarter southward, is VEN DEN DE PA ROL JEW LE JAH."

They say, "We are four of the holy and mighty Angels of God, sent from before his throne, to pass and repass through the four quarters of the earth; and many are the holy angels that bear us company. And thus shall we visit the earth in partial silence, as this Roll goes forth, until we have marked the door posts of all, as our God hath commanded, who shall humble themselves and repent at his word, by proclaiming a solemn fast, and cease from their awful crimes of wickedness, and turn to him in righteousness."

Such is the character of the book which this eccentric people attempt to impose upon the world as a revelation from God. At first it would seem strange that the ministry should think to humbug mankind with such matter.

It will be remembered that the title page speaks of this book as being in two parts. The first part only has been given to the public. And this only have I noticed. The second part is somewhat different from this; but makes no less pretentions to divine inspiration. It professes to be a sort of testimony, confirmatory of the first. When the first part had been read throughout the denomination, all the members who were competent were required by the ministry to write a testimony concerning it. The ministry having collected together all these, made selections from the mass to compose the second part; which if I recollect aright, is a volume something larger than the first. The first contains 222 pages royal octavo. The second part is printed and circulated to a certain extent in the society, two copies being allowed to every family. One being deposited with the elder, and the other with the eldress. Those who are considered good Shakers can get permission of their *lead* to read this volume. But considerable caution is observed to prevent any wicked worldling from seeing it. Having obtained permission to read it, I improved the opportunity to make large extracts from it. Why this volume is kept back from the public does not appear. Probably some of the influential members saw the folly of publishing such a work as is contained in these two volumes; were not able to prevent the publishing of the first part, but hindered the second. However this may be, I shall take the liberty, as it professes to be a revelation from God, not to the Shakers exclusively, but to mankind at large, to notice it. If it truly came from God, I shall be responsible to him for showing it to the world before the time; (unless indeed the time be fully come.) If it be a fraud, I claim the right to expose it. And that it is a fraud I have no doubt. Inasmuch as they have sent forth the first part, why should they keep back the second part, which confirms the first? *I deny their right to keep back God's word from a perishing world.* And without further explanation proceed with my extracts.

Extracts from the second part of the Sacred Roll.

Which professes to contain " The testifying seals of some of the ancient prophets and holy angels, with the testimonies of living witnesses."

I quote a single paragraph from the preface.

" The inspired writers and testators of the word contained in this second part, have consented to the publication of the same, only in compliance with the requirement of God, feeling it a duty to acknowledge his mercy and goodness in this the fourth and last dispensation of his grace to man."

I shall make as brief extracts as I can and give an idea of the character of the book. I shall commence with quoting a single paragraph from what is denominated

" THE TESTIFYING SEAL OF THE PROPHET JEREMIAH."

Fifth paragraph. " Therefore hearken, O ye nations of the earth, and listen all ye people, to this his Sacred Roll, as the voice of the living God in solemn warning and tender love; and if you believe the words which I spake in days of old, believe me now, when I say that this Sacred and Divine Roll which is now sent forth unto you is not the work of the vain and aspiring imagination of fallen man : but was directed by the holy spirit of the Lord your God, and contains those solemn truths to which every soul must bow, or finally fail of his protection and blessing; for he hath not sent forth his word in vain, nor will he strive with man for nought."

(Signed) " Inspired writer,"
" WILLIAM TRIPURE."

Dated " Canterbury, N. H."

The next is from "THE PROPHET ELISHA."
I extract the 15th paragraph. "The earth shall yet be in commotion, the fire of the ever blessed Gospel, taught by my faithful Son, your blessed Savior, and revived through my anointing goodness, by the Mother of the New creation, Ann Lee, shall burn and run as flaming fire among stubble; and souls shall be awakened by the sound of the heavenly harpers, harping with their harps; yea, by my holy and proclaiming angels whom I will send to pass and repass through the earth, sounding the cheering trumpet of sweet liberty to the soul bound in sin, and to the seekers after true righteousness.
"Canterbury, N. H." and signed "Inspired writer, Hester Adams."
The following is taken entire and needs no comment.

TESTIMONY OF ELEVEN MIGHTY ANGELS, THAT ATTENDED THE WRITING OF THE ROLL.

Given by Inspiration, February 16, 1843.

I, the Holy Angel of Almighty Power, by name, Al' sign te' re Jah,' do witness and testify that the word of the Lord has been correctly written by mortal hand.

I the holy angel of the Lord, do solemnly affirm that the word which has long been concealed from mortal eyes, is now revealed by Almighty power, and made plain to mortal view.

I, the holy proclaiming angel of the Lord, do solemnly testify that it has been through deep tribulation, and as heavy sorrow, and suffering as mortal clay, or the inhabitant thereof, was able to endure, that the word of the Lord has been obtained and correctly written by mortal hand, for mortal eyes to view.

I, the mighty Angel of the Lord, by name Con' sole te re Jah mon' shue, do solemnly testify that my eyes have beheld the word of the Lord correctly written by mortal hand; and it is in truth the invariable word of the Lord, which will stand unalterable through time and in eternity.

I, the holy proclaiming angel of truth, do firmly testify, that it is the word of the Lord, which has been written by mortal hand; and should any one put forth a hand to destroy it, or alter in the least degree, either by adding to, or diminishing it, that soul shall surely fall by the sword of his displeasure, and drink of his furious wrath and indignation.

I, an Angel of Mighty power, do testify, that the inspired writer of the Roll was chosen by the Lord Almighty to write his sacred word; and the will of his God he has done, and his duty faithfully executed.

I, a mighty Angel of glory, do firmly declare the word to be true that the forementioned angels have testified.

I, a Mighty Angel of the Lord, do solemnly protest, that not one promise of God, stated in his sacred Roll, and Book, shall fail, or pass away, but shall be fulfilled, even to a jot and tittle.

I, a mighty Angel of warning, do solemnly affirm that the anger of a justly provoked God is greatly kindled against the inhabitants of earth; and he is about to visit her in the fury of his wrath and displeasure, and cut down her inhabitants in judgment, if they hearken not to his warning voice of mercy.

I, a Holy Angel of the Lord, do solemnly declare, that within the covers of this Sacred book, is inserted the word of the Lord correctly written by mortal hand, which has been done in the true fear of God; and let all who peruse it, do it, in a measure of the same holy fear in which it was given. For I will ever stand as a witness of the usage of the Sacred Roll; and with a just reward will I meet every soul when they have done with time.

I, a mighty Angel of the Lord, by name Pre' line fi' nan vas' ten va, ren ve' ne do firmly testify that we, the Holy Angels, have witnessed the contents of this Roll correctly written; and the word inserted therein is the word of that God who created and knoweth all things; though plain, yet it is true; then let every soul remember, that whom the Father loveth, He chasteneth; and will kindly warn them to flee from the dangers that shall come.

Hear my word and obey the same, crieth the voice of him who sitteth on high, and ruleth over all. Inspired Witness." Harriot Goodwin.

I can here testify, that the foregoing statements are no fiction, or vain imagination. But I have an evidence within my own heart, beyond all wavering, or caviling feelings whatever, that it is truth and reality, that the Lord's time has fully come for his warning voice of mercy to be sounded throughout the four quarters of the earth; that he may gather the wheat into his garners, while He separateth the chaff therefrom, and burneth it with unquenchable fire; for saith God, unto him that seeketh mercy aright, I will show mercy; and crieth the Holy angels of mercy, whithersoever the word of the Lord Almighty goeth, there shall we go, and whosoever shall hearken and obey it, the same shall be blessed, but whosoever shall destroy or treat it with scorn, or ridicule, the same shall be cursed.

These things have been made plain to my view as the natural elements above, or the inhabitants of earth below; therefore, it would be as reasonable for me to dispute my existence, as to dispute the reality of them. I, therefore, stand as a witness before God and all men, through time and in eternity, that it is in truth and reality, the word of the one only true living God which is contained in the pages of this Sacred book.

New Lebanon, N. Y., February 18, 1843. Harriet Goodwin, Born June 2d, 1823; and was brought by her parents into the United Society, at New Lebanon, December 19, 1833.

The following communication from the same author and extracted from the same source, taken with the above, shows her to be a young woman of fine talents. A powerful imagination, and excellent expression. Limited as must have been her advantages for intellectual culture, it is not saying too much, that nature has endowed her with a brilliant mind. Pity it should be devoted to upholding that stupendous fraud, Shakerism. But she is harnessed in, and *must* move with the rest. Herein Shakerdom is her home, her all. Here she is surrounded with all the mighty influences of wealth, powerful friends, and relations. Those who assume in the most solemn manner, to have been appointed by God to direct her whole life here; and all the influences they are capable of exerting, are used to make her feel that her immortal happiness depends upon her implicit obedience to all they require. It is so not only in her case but in all other cases. And they are strangers when out of the society. More peculiar to their own countrymen than foreigners are. Here is the very life of Shakerism. It is very difficult for those who go there in childhood to break away from these influences. And it is not strange in view of these facts, that the " Lead" as they call themselves, should be able to make her or others instrumental in promoting their views and purposes, whether they be good, or bad. But I will proceed with my extracts.

TESTIMONY OF HARRIET GOODWIN, OF NEW LEBANON, N. Y., Sabbath morning, July tenth, eighteen hundred and forty-two, I saw, placed on the top of the dwelling-house, a beautiful sign; it reached the whole length of the house, and appeared to be about six feet wide. I could not at that time see any writing on the sign, it shone with such very great brightness. It resembled the color of gold.

At first I was struck with fear at the sight, I supposed it to be placed there by mortal hand. But I soon beheld three mighty angels guarding it; I then knew it to be something placed there by a supernatural power.

On Saturday evening following, July 16th, I again beheld the same. On Sabbath morning 17th, it was again made plain to my view, so that I could behold many of the letters; but I could not read it. On the evening of the same day, after retiring to rest, I suddenly heard a voice sounding in my ears like peals of mighty thunder, which caused me to fear exceedingly; saying, Keep silent, O thou worm of the dust; for lo, I am the Almighty, who is able, in the twinkling of an eye, to crush that soul in atoms, who dares presume to make mention of my doings, before my time hath fully come. But lo, In my Zion have I placed my name, forevermore to stand; there have I made myself known; and from Zion shall my light and glory shine forth, through out the whole earth. The dwellings of my people shall I cause to glow with beauty, and upon their high towers, and most sacred places will I place my name, word and will; and from thence shall the same go forth to the nations of the earth, while millions, from both far and near, shall flock together to behold my word, and admire, with astonishment and fear, the wonderful and marvellous doings of my all righteous hand; while the scoffer and mocker, I will lay low before Me, and cause them to howl with agony; and the filthy and unclean I will scourge and abuse.

Behold, O thou babe in Israel, thou hast this day, in very deed, beheld, in a small measure, the doings of my hand; but small it is to what your eyes shall yet behold; for Lo, I am the Almighty Creator of heaven and earth; therefore great and wonderful is and shall be, the work of my hand. *Here the word finished for this time.*

On Thursday evening following, July twenty-first, after retiring to rest, I heard a trumpet sounded very loud and solemn, but heard not a word spoken; yet I knew it to be from one of the guardian Angels on the house. I then turned my eyes towards the sound, and again beheld the sign; but could not yet behold a word on it.

On the fourth day of August, I again heard the trumpet of one of the mighty Angels sounding; which was truly solemn and heavenly. I looked towards the sign, and beheld it much plainer than I ever had before; and could once in a while distinguish a letter, from amidst the dazzling brightness that surrounded it; and at length I could possibly discern a few words, written towards the bottom of it, which were as follows:

Lo! lo! I am the Almighty, the ever existing and never ending; holding in my right hand, the sword of my judgment and displeasure, and in my left, the vial of my wrath and indignation, with which I shall shortly visit the earth, and release her from the heavy weight under which she is now groaning.

I will not always strive to no purpose ; I will not always threaten and not perform ; I will no longer be blasphemed and mocked by the vile, the filthy, and unclean. Here in my Zion have I placed my name, here are the chosen of my delight, my holy, holy people; and from thence shall my word go forth ; and he that heareth it, and obeyeth it not, shall fall by the sword of my displeasure.

On Sabbath afternoon, August 7th, I again beheld the sign, and heard one of the Angels speak the following words : Behold, even seven times have passed by, and thou, O little one, hast been called to behold and witness this, the word of the Almighty. But rest assured, that thou hast not beheld, but in a small measure, that which is now placed upon the dwelling of the righteous.

But the word of thy God and my God, is this day fulfilled and obeyed ; which was, that I, the Holy Angel of Almighty power, should not rest, until seven times I had called forth the least child in this part of his zion, whose eyes had beheld the glory of God, and whose lips had been moved to sound forth his sacred word ; that she might stand as a witness of his marvellous doings. But yet louder crieth the voice of Him who sitteth on high, O Mi kh' lon se vin' da ; rest shall not crown thy spirit, nor peace and quietness prevail around thee, until my word be fully known and my righteous law fulfiled.

Even seven times shalt thou sound thy trumpet of alarm, and call forth him in whom I take pleasure ; who has, through sufferings sore, and sorrow deep, washed his garment white, and found favor in my sight ; for lo, he shall suffer even as did my first begotten Son, many things for my name's-sake, and the Gospel's.

And on the sixth time that thou shalt call him forth, I will draw nigh, and crown him with wisdom, and clothe him with power ; and cause his eyes to open, that he shall see my glory, and the word of his God ; and write in full concerning the same.

And on the seventh time he shall behold the whole, and write the same, and, at that time, I will cause four thousand of my most holy Angels to be present, and witness my word correctly written. For lo, I will have witnesses, both in heaven and on earth; but through sufferings deep shall my word be obtained, and in tribulation shall it be written. The voice then ceased, and the Holy Angel turned to me and said; Little one, hast thou not heard the voice of Almighty power? I answered, yea. Then go ye, and correctly write all that has passed in these seven interviews, and I will be with thee to help thee. But remember, I shall call forth many witnesses, ere the day cometh when mortal eyes shall behold the word of the Lord written plain to be understood by the inhabitants of the earth.

Sabbath afternoon, August 14th, eighteen hundred and forty-two, while in meeting, I saw a Holy and mighty Angel enter the meeting room, He marched to the head of the room, and placed his wings upon many of the brethren and sisters, saying ; Arise, arise, and witness for me ; for lo I am an Angel of Almighty power, sent from the throne of God to guard his heritage, his Zion on earth.

And surely great is my mission, and marvellous shall be my word and work ; therefore, I call you to arise and witness for me, with many others; for know ye, I shall work in the sight of man, and of the children of this world ; and many things will I make plain to their view, and bring to their understanding. And not seven and a half times shall pass away, before they shall hear my voice, and acknowledge the goodness of their God, and behold his name printed on Zion, where He has placed it, forever more to stand. The Angel then disappeared, and I saw him no more at that time.

After meeting was closed, as I was returning home, feeling entirely free from the burden which I had previously felt, I was met by the Angel after I entered the dwelling.; his wings were raised, and his countenance shone with great brightness, yet it was solemn and serene ; which struck me with reverence and awe, insomuch that I had scarcely strength to stand. The Angel looked at me in a very sacred and solemn manner, and bid me follow him back into the meeting-room, which I did; and there I found one of the sisters; he then placed my hand in hers, and bid me walk with her and sing a little solemn song which he sung; this I did.

After walking a few moments, the angel said to this certain sister, I would that thou, little one, learn this song and sing with me. I am an Angel of Almighty power, and have come unto thee, clothed in thy Mother's spirit; and this is thy Mother's song of mourning, for surely she mourneth and weepeth for Zion, because great and heavy will yet be her tribulation; and her children will yet mourn and weep, in very deed with her.

The Angel then desired to march this song throughout the dwelling-house, through every hall, and every retiring room, that all might feel the spirit of their Mother, and sense in a small measure, a degree of her tribulation; which was done. The Angel then entered one of the rooms where several were assembled, and turning to the one whom his God has chosen to write the Sacred Bible, he said; O thou beloved one, prepare thy heart for tribulation; great has been, and great shall be thy tribulation.

The Angel then proceeded through the house, and after returning to the place where he had previously been speaking, he spoke the following words.

O Holy Anointed, and dearly beloved, have not tribulation and persecution been the lot of God's people in Zion through all past ages? and hath not the Lord promised protection to them in obedience? Surely he has, and will fulfil according to his promise.

I am an Angel of Almighty power sent from the throne of God, bearing on my wings a Heavenly cross, and it is the will of thy God that the cross be placed on my chosen instruments. Wilt thou not, O thou little one, take this cross from off my shoulders? He replied, the will of my God be done.

"Also upon my head is placed, a solemn and weighty Roll, containing The words of the Lord thy God, which has been written with his own finger, and places on this thy dwelling place, for nations to behold; yea, that which shall yet be proclaimed in the earth.

And lo, I say unto you, It has been through tribulation deep, that this word has been handed forth; and in and through tribulation deep, and sufferings sore, shall it be obtained and written by mortal hand, for nations to behold. Even seven times have I called thee forth, O thou little one, to view this my word, and the word of thy God, though not through my loud and solemn trumpet, therefore, thou hast not heard me in full. But yet seven times more will I again call thee forth to read this solemn and sacred word before thou shalt write it, but on the sixth time thou shalt write concerning it, and on the seventh thou shalt write the whole.

Yea, even as the Lord did place a rainbow in the heavens, as a sign and sure promise unto Noah, that He would never again destroy the earth, or the inhabitants thereof, by floods of water; so shall the doings of my hand which ye have seen, stand as a sign unto his people, that ye have this day received his holy, and sacred word, which shall yet be written by mortal hand, and made plain to mortal eyes; and be understood by many of the inhabitants of the earth.

"I have now finished the word which my Heavenly Father gave me to speak, but I leave you not at present, nay, I the Holy Angel will remain with this little one, even Philemon, until this work is accomplished, and the word is finished, saith the Holy Angel.

NOTE. The inspired writer of this Roll and Book had been shown by an Angel, at times, for more than two years previous, that God had a word direct to the nations of the earth; but in what way it should be sent forth, it had never been shown me.

The Angel repeatedly informed me that God would direct and conduct this work in his own time and according to his own will and pleasure. These things I kept and pondered in my own heart, until God should make his own time known entirely according to his own will. Of these things the inspired writer of this communication, knew nothing, as I had kept them entirely within myself.

PHILOMON STEWART.

January first, eighteen hundred forty three, I heard a heavenly trumpet very loudly sounding. I listened, and the sound ceased; I paused for a moment, when I again heard it, which seemed to cause the regions above to shake with terror.

I then looked towards the Northwest, and there beheld a beautiful rainbow; and on the rainbow stood four thousand holy and mighty angels, each holding in his right hand a flaming sword, and in his left, a vial of God's wrath and indignation. I gazed on the scene, with admiration and reverence, yet feared exceedingly.

I again heard the heavenly trumpeters loudly sounding their solemn trumpets, which caused the arches of heaven to echo; and at every blast I was struck with exceeding great fear and terror. I then heard a solemn and heavenly song sung, which was played upon instruments of music, by forty and four of the most holy angels that marched in front.

They moved along slowly, while the rainbow still continued under their feet, until they reached the dwelling house, where the Roll or Sacred Sheet was spread. Then did the ninety and nine trumpet-sounding Angels raise their trumpets, and loudly blow a solemn blast, which they repeated fourteen times; signifying that for fourteen days they would all attend to the writing of the Roll.

Then spake one of the mighty Angels, saying; For fourteen days shall we, the holy Angels of Almighty power, tarry with the son of man and inspire him with wisdom, light and understanding, that he may behold the glory of his God, and do his all righteous will. Yea, we will open the eyes of his soul, and give unto him true knowledge and understanding; that he may, if he will, correctly write the word and do the will of his All-wise and All-powerful Creator.

But let him not fear to write it in full, exact and correct that every nation may know that God is a God of justice; impartial and merciful. And moreover I say, if he writeth not the word in full, but keepeth back a part, fearing man, and the powers of earth, rather than his God; I say, and understand ye; more tolerable was it, in ancient date, for the inhabitants of Sodom and Gomorrah, than it will be for him. Far better would it have been, had he never existed on the earth; or, that a millstone be hung about his neck, and he be cast into the sea, than that he should see the days that he shall live to see.

But if he obeyeth the voice of his Father which is in Heaven, all shall be well with him. Though man be mighty, yet God is Almighty; though man be able to torture and perplex, yet God is able, in the twinkling of an eye, to crush and lay low the haughtiness of man, and raise up and exalt the humble seeker after true righteousness. Therefore fear exceedingly; yea, tremble with fear.

Then the forty and four holy Angels, taking hold of the sheet, raised it up and said unto me, Look, behold and see, O thou babe in Israel, the word and doings of thy All-wise Creator. I looked and beheld the word of the Lord written in full, for the first time. It was written upon a sheet which to my view, appeared like fire, and the letters were as letters of gold. And after the angels had raised it up, about six feet from the roof of the house, taking it in the middle, it was then shown to me as I had before seen it, in the shape of a sign; the sheet was again spread, and I beheld it in full.

Then said the Angel; A time and a half a time, and a half of a half a time, shall in no wise pass away, nay, the sun shall not reach its meridian height at noon-day, nor the moon spread her gentle beams of light over you by night, even ninety and nine times, before ye shall behold the word of the Lord your God written in full, by mortal hand, and made plain to the view of the inhabitants of Zion.

Then did they roll up the Roll, and seal it with the ninety and nine seals; and singing a song of rejoicing, and playing the same upon their instruments, they marched into the upper hall in the dwelling house, laid down the Roll, and vanished out of my sight.

January twenty second, eighteen hundred and forty

three, I again beheld the four thousand Angels approach the place of worship, with quickened steps; and as they entered, I heard a band of heavenly music, which sounded in my ears like many harpers playing upon their harps. Then the Angels raised their solemn trumpets and gave a solemn blast; then said they, Peace be unto the righteous; yea, peace, joy and tranquility shall crown the days, and rest in the bosoms of the true and upright soldiers of Christ.

But woe, woe, and a heavy woe, shall rest upon that soul that shall presume to make mention of the doings of their God to the children of darkness before the time hath fully come, when his word He will reveal, and his will he will make known, in his own time and season, way and manner. Even of these, the vials of God's wrath and indignation, which we hold in our left hands, (and with which he hath purposed to visit the earth and the inhabitants thereof,) shall they constantly drink; and as a dead and lifeless branch, shall they fall from the tree of life, to rise no more, through time or in eternity.

The Angels then formed a circle around the chosen instrument, and said; Thou child of sorrow prepare thyself for death; for a sacrifice of all things, even to the laying down of thy life, doth thy God require! Thy path is paved with tribulation; therefore, in the bitterest of grief, the heaviest of sorrow and keenest of tribulation, shalt thou walk by day and by night till thou art willing to sacrifice all to thy God, that thou mayest be able to know and do his will:

For never again will the Lord condescend to reveal his all-righteous will unto mortals, unless through tribulation, sorrow and grief, they have washed their garments white, and in the lowest of humility have bowed their spirits, and opened the door of their hearts with thankfulness and resignation, that he might enter and work.

We say not that the Lord requires you to give up your natural life; but he requires a willingness to sacrifice all things, even unto death. The Angels then sounded their trumpets, and I saw them no more at that time.

Early on the morning of the first day of February, eighteen hundred and forty three, I was awakened from my sleep, hearing the Angels again sounding their trumpets, and the forty and four most holy angels playing upon their instruments of music. I looked towards the west and again beheld the sheet spread. The Angels then raised their wings with joy, and loudly rung their bells of alarm; shouted a shout of rejoicing, and sung a solemn song of praise, saying;

Rejoice, O Zion; let thy inhabitants be joyful, and let joy and rejoicing prevail throughout thy borders. For lo, this day will the Lord of Heaven draw nigh, and clothe with wisdom and crown with strength, that soul who has, in sufferings and sorrow, laid himself low before God, even to dust, that he might find favor in his sight, and be able to do his holy will. This day will he commence revealing that which has long been concealed; and this day shall long be remembered by thee, O Zion.

I did not hear or see any more at that time. But on the morning of the second day of February, I again heard the Angels sound their trumpets, and saw them take the sheet, and again roll it up and seal it, even with ninety and nine seals; they then carried it into the room where it was to be written, unsealed and placed it upon the wall.

Then said the Angels to the chosen instrument, O thou child of sorrow, this day do we, the mighty and proclaiming, Angels of the Lord, commence tarrying with thee, to feed and support thee, and to witness the word of the Lord correctly copied from this sacred sheet, by mortal hand for mortal eyes to view; for this was thy Father's command, and this is our mission. He chooseth witnesses, both in the heavens and on the earth; for out of the mouths of many witnesses shall his word be established.

On the fourth day of February, eighteen hundred and forty three, I saw the instrument that was to write the Roll, go into his room, and the four hundred Angels follow him; and after he had commenced writing, I saw the Angels place a seal on every page as he wrote it, as their witness and testimony that it was correctly written.

On the fifth of February, I saw yet another sheet placed upon the house top, resembling the first, having the same word written upon it; and I saw an angel standing at the top of it, having a head like a lion, and wings like an angel. And as the Instrument copied the word correctly, from the Roll, the Angel blotted it out.

On the ninth of February, I saw the Angels ascend even unto the throne of the Almighty, and there gather food, strength and blessing for the Instrument; and with it I saw them feed him; saying, be faithful thou little one, even as thou hast been; for lo, thy God, thy Father and eternal Maker, is well pleased with thee.

On the sixteenth of February, I again heard the Angels sounding their trumpets; saying, Well done thou good and faithful servant, enter thou into the joy of thy Lord. Well be it with thee, because of thy obedience; because thou hast faithfully done the will, and correctly written the word of thy Father which is in heaven. And whosoever shall put forth their hand to destroy it, shall fall by the sword of his displeasure, and be banished from his presence. The Angels soon disappeared, and I saw them no more.

Testimony of Martha Van Valen.

On Saturday evening, December seventeenth, one thousand eight hundred and forty-two, while in meeting, I saw a very powerful angel enter the east side of the room, clothed in shining brightness. His appearance filled my soul with godly fear. He said to me, I am the angel of Eternal Truth. Look thou! behold this Roll, which shall be written in my time. I looked and saw a very lengthy Roll held before me, and it was sealed with many seals.

The angel broke the first seal, and commenced unrolling it. He unrolled a part, and then came to another seal. In this manner he continued unrolling and breaking the seals, until it was all unrolled. And by the space it covered in the room, it must have been about twenty feet long, and several feet wide. I saw it was covered with writing, but could not read one word of it.

Sabbath morning December eighteenth, while in our morning meeting, I saw the same angel with the same Roll; and he held it before me. At this time a very solemn feeling came over me, accompanied with a weight of tribulation. There was also another spirit standing by me; and I said, what does this mean? Is this for me to read? Nay, said the spirit, it is not for you to read; but it is the eternal word of God, and will be written and sent to all nations of the earth. You will yet know this to be true.

The angel with the Roll now left the room, and I looked to see where he went; and I saw him go towards New Lebanon. My impression then was, that the Roll was to be written there, and sent forth as I had been told. This I mentioned to some of the family at the time.

The next day I saw the Roll again, and the angel that unrolled and unsealed it as before. I did not count the number of the seals, neither did I know their meaning.

Tuesday afternoon, April fourth, one thousand eight hundred and forty-three, a mighty angel appeared to me. He first told his name, Ha la vae tha na; and then said, O thou little one, bow before me.

The appearance of this mighty angel was majestic and solemn. When he spake his voice caused me to tremble with godly fear and reverence. After a pause, he said; Bow down thou mortal instrument, bow low, low, even to the dust of the earth, if thou wilt become a witness to the truth of the holy word of God, which in his wisdom he hath seen fit to cause to be written. Yea, the word of your Eternal Parents hath been revealed by a mighty and powerful angel; and written by mortal hand at New Lebanon, the Mount of God.

O ye witnesses of the eternal word which is about to be sent forth to the different nations of the earth, through the mercy, power and wisdom of God, have ye not felt the solemn and awful weight of the word and work which have been revealed in the Zion of God upon earth? Can you not testify, in truth, that the Lord God hath declared, through his ministering angels, that the fire of his Almighty truth should be spread through earth's remotest bounds? Yea, to this, and to more can ye bear witness. Hark, hear the awful sound; Woe! woe! woe! awful woes are pronounced upon the inhabitants of the earth. A sign shall be given in the east. Terrible and mighty is the army that shall be sent to and fro in the earth, with vials filled with the wrath of God, to pour upon the proud, the high, the unjust, the unmerciful, the filthy worker, and those who regard not the laws of God or man.

All those who will trifle with, or in any way abuse, destroy or cause to be destroyed, the sacred words of truth written and sent forth to all the nations of the earth, by the command of the great Jehovah, better, far better would it be for them, if they had never been born. For, saith the Eternal God, I will meet those that do this thing with heavy judgments. My words to them shall be like the roarings of mighty thunders; and no forgiveness shall they find, but through heavy sufferings. So take warning and be careful, O ye children of earth, how you treat that which you do not understand.

To all who are called to witness to this, the word of your God, know ye, there will disputers and cavilers arise, but fear them not; for what is written is the word of your God, and all the powers of darkness will never be able to destroy the truth thereof; but it will stand to the endless ages of eternity.

Inspired Witness,
MARTHA VAN VALEN.

As a witness, I boldly and firmly declare to all mankind, that what is here written is no fiction, but is the everlasting truth. It is simply what I saw and heard.

I was born in Fishkill, Dutchess County, State of New York, May first, eighteen hundred four; came here to live, April, eighteen hundred and thirty-three.

MARTHA VAN VALEN.
Hancock, Mass., April 4, 1843.

Extracts from Adah Zillah Potter's eight interviews with the angel " Mane Mirah Vak na Sina Jah." These interviews were held on the 22d Jan. 1842, evening—Feb. 5th, 1842, ten o'clock Morn.—Feb. 21st, 1842, Morn.—March 1, 1842, Morn.—March 12, 1842. May 1, 1842, while assembled with others on the Holy Mount. July 6, 1842, Morn.—July 7, 1842, awakened just as the clock struck three. The account of these interviews cover 16 closely printed octavo pages. And all evidently the outpourings of a strong and wonderfully excited imagination. It is perhaps, taken as a whole, rather a strong specimen of the visions and revelations common among the people since 1837. But taken with the others given it is a fair one. I make brief extracts.

The angel signs his name, as given above, to several of the communications given.

In the third interview she describes the angel as he appeared to her, as follows.

The voice now ceased speaking, and I beheld in the east, an angel moving slowly along, and soon came very near. The appearance was solemn and terrible; for the body, from the neck, was like that of a mighty man, and the head was like that of an eagle. He had four exceedingly large wings, two upon each shoulder; these were open and spread each way.

The feet were like the feet of an elephant, and seemed to be well shod with cast iron; in the right hand was a very large Roll, sealed with ninety-nine seals; and in the left a book, the lids or cover of which, was of some kind of metal, but I did not know what; and it was clasped together with a clasp of steel. I feared but spoke not, for I knew not what to say; indeed I dared not speak.

The mighty angel now spoke to me in a voice like thunder, and said, Me, ye now hear and see, and ye know that I am; and from this time ye will not often hear me, though ye may see yet again and again, for I am indeed the power. But the voice that ye shall hear, ye shall not know, neither shall ye see from whence it proceedeth until it shall come. * * *

The angel now held forth, *first* the Roll, and *then* the book; and said, The time will surely come, and is not far distant, but is not yet.

But alas! alas! *Se a na qua, e fa ma.* Lo, these days in which that righteous God of never ending charity, has now winked at the pretended ignorance and hard understanding of the children of men, and even of his own people, and hath showed mercy unto all, will be numbered and will pass away.

In the fifth interview at the close, the angel says,

And let it be remembered, that my word is not exclusively to one part, nor to another part of Zion's inhabitants; but to every part, and to the nations abroad the same. But now, my last word unto thee, O thou mortal child, that hast these five times listened to me, and to the voice that abideth with me, is this:

Thou shalt in no wise provide for thyself any article of any kind, whereon to write my word; but as I shall command thee, so shalt thou do. Upon thy knees shalt thou place the Holy Bible, (for that is the most sacred and holy word now known among the children of men;) and upon that thou shalt write, all that I shall command thee.

And that sign shall stand as a lasting memorial of my eternal power, within Zion, for generations to come; and no name, save Ma ne Mi rah Vak ne Si na Jah, shall be upon my word.

This is the end of my word for this time; I go now, yet come again in season; but not as I am now; but number my times, and keep my time, and be a ready witness for me. Amen.

Ma ne Mi rah Vak ne Si na Jah.

In perfect obedience to the word of the angel, I did write every word of it upon a Bible, only five and a half inches wide, and nine in length, which I laid upon my knees. And though many asked me why I did so, yet I told no one, until I had finished. I have now done all that I am as yet required to do; and to the whole communication I freely and confidently sign my name.

Adah Zillah Potter.

At the close of these interviews the writer says,

I have now nothing more to say, save only that I saw the mighty angel with the mortal writer of the foregoing Roll, several times, while writing the book. And it is with a degree of pleasure that I add my testimony to the truth and reality of the whole word and work; and can readily hand forth this statement, as a witnessing word, in obedience to the word of the holy angel. And now, this whole word, I am willing and ready to seal with my life, or in whatever manner it may please a just and holy God to require of me. ADAH ZILLAH POTTER.
New Lebanon, Columbia County, State of New York, April, 1843.

Testimony of Joseph Wicker. About 9 o'clock, this evening, (April 20, 1843,) while engaged in prayer and supplication to God, I received a small roll; and it was said to me, This is the word of the Lord. After receiving it, I returned it to the Angel who brought it, and I was required to write while he read, as follows: Thus saith the Lord who upholdeth the righteous, and saith to Zion, Receive my word that I now send unto thee. My word is truth, and it shall not return unto Me void, but the word I have spoken, I will surely perform; and I will empty out the wicked, who despise judgment, and scoff at my holy givings. In mercy have I now sent forth my word anew unto the inhabitants of the earth; and I have again set life and death before them, Teaching them plainly, what I require of the souls I have created, and warning them of the judgments which shall shortly pass through the earth, and enter the habitations of the sons and daughters of pride, who have chosen the paths of iniquity, and the seal of destruction. So from my Holy Mount, from the center of the Zion of my likeness on earth, have I caused this my word to go forth; and in truth and faithfulness have I caused it to be plainly written, that all who desire it, may clearly understand how to find my mercy and forgiveness.

O, ye inhabitants of the earth, is it a strange thing, that I am able now as in days of old, to make known my word unto you, through the means of my own choosing? is my power diminished, so that I cannot reveal my word to souls who dwell in tabernacles of clay? Who hath taken from Me, or, who hath removed my attributes? Will ye set bounds for Me, that I cannot pass, or determine, what thing I shall not do? When did I ever teach you that I would never again speak unto the sons of men?

If ye would be wise, receive my testimonies which I have revealed in this day of my favor, and kindness unto sinful man, and reject not my laws.

INSPIRED WITNESS,

JOSEPH WICKER.

Strange as the contents of the foregoing pages may appear to the natural man, I feel no hesitation to declare my faith in the truth of the doctrines, warnings, invitations, and instructions, set forth and inculcated in them; and that they are of Divine origin, and eminently calculated to produce peace and happiness in all who observe and keep them.

I was born in the Town and County of Bennington, State of Vermont, March 23, 1790; was gathered into the Society in April, 1806.

JOSEPH WICKER.

Hancock, Berkshire County, State of Massachusetts, April 20, 1843.

A Short Communication from a Holy Spirit.

RECEIVED AT UNION VILLAGE, WARREN COUNTY, OHIO, May 14, 1843.

Thus saith the Spirit; O, my children, unite your souls as the heart of one, and move forward with the increasing work of God. Marvellous and great are the mysteries revealed in this your day; for truly the Lord hath made known his will and word to his people on earth, and will declare the same to all nations and people, in his own time.

Marvel not, though I tell you I have been a witness of the Holy word of God, revealed to mortal clay, which must shortly be given to the rulers of the land, and to the nations afar off.*

But know ye, when a living testimony hath gone forth from Zion, then shall tribulation be fully realized among God's chosen people; therefore, stand ye firm and strong, and fear not what an unbelieving world may inflict upon you. But keep ye low and quiet; stand firm and unshaken, amidst storms and tribulation, for the Holy hand of God will cover and protect his chosen, from every harm; Zion shall flourish, bloom and grow, like a well watered garden; her beauty and glory shall spread far and wide; and many shall flock to her peaceful borders to learn the Holy way of righteousness.

Then O ye children, how necessary it is, that you keep your stores full, and your souls well supplied with the beautiful gifts of God; for they will adorn the soul with heavenly beauty and glory; yea, and your light shall shine forth like the morning sun; and all who behold it shall say, Behold the light and glory of Zion! the beautiful city of God, where dwell peace and righteousness, abounding with the blessings of heaven forevermore.

Now, saith the Spirit, I have not much to say at this time, but I have a little anthem which I will give you; that you may know that the Lord is visiting the earth, in mercy and in judgment.

Anthem.

Lo, the Angel of the Lord is swiftly flying over the earth; sounding, sounding, through his holy trumpet, saying, Hear, O hear ye my warning voice! For lo, the God of Heaven, clothed with might and power, is descending in mercy and in judgment; and He will smite the inhabitants of the earth with sore and heavy judgments, for the wickedness thereof is very great.

Then, O ye children of his Holy name; O ye se ve' se, li ne voo', be ye lowly; for the humble, the Holy and pure,

* NOTE. The inspired writer had no knowledge of this Roll and Book, only by Divine revelation, at the time the above was written.

shall abide in the day of God's visitation, for they are his faithful servants, marked with his Holy name. Then fear ye not, ye lovely chosen of your God; for ye shall be as an ensign lifted up, and as a banner of pure light; for, saith the Lord, whose ways are just and true, I will be your God, and ye shall be my O' le an sa voo' and my celes' ta, li la va.' I will guide and comfort you, through all scenes of tribulation, and you shall be the jewels of my Holy love, and the glory of my righteous name, protected by my Holy hand forevermore.

A Seal from the Lord Jehovah.

Read by a Holy Angel, and copied by inspiration, at Union Village, Warren County, Ohio, June 26, 1843; as an evidence of the truth and correctness of the Great Roll, which was written in his own name for the nations of the earth, and which has been correctly copied through deep tribulation, by a mortal instrument of God's own choosing, at the Holy Mount.

I Am that I Am. Before me there was not, and above me there is none; And behold, out of thy mouth has gone forth my everlasting commandment, and the word of Eternal Truth; to which no mortal clay shall add, neither shall they diminish, unless they are anointed of my Holy Spirit and commanded so to do.

For I have spoken it in my wisdom, according as I have intended; and let no one that is ever blessed with a privilege of reading, or hearing this Sacred Word of mine, suffer themselves to cavil, or yield to an unbelieving spirit, and doubt of its Divine origin.

I say, be careful that you do not suffer yourselves to harbor such feelings; for great will be the blasphemy of all such as do this; and sore will be my judgments that shall fall upon them, to humble them low to the dust, till they shall know that I am the Holy and righteous God of Zion, against whom no man shall raise his voice, or put forth his hand, and prosper; but every soul shall bow before Me, in low humiliation, and bend their knees in humble prayer; and with their own tongues confess in the presence of my witnesses, the evils which they have done, or never see my kingdom in peace.

I will deal with every soul in righteousness, according to their works; and blessed shall be the humble soul, that will come at the call of mercy, and bow down to seek a place in my Holy Zion; and not wait to be driven by judgments, to seek a refuge and a hiding place.

For lo, in the day when the earth shall be visited with famine and desolation, and many sore judgments which I will send; and when my Holy Angels shall blow their trumpets like many mighty thunders, to awaken those who are resting in their sins, then shall the nations of the earth tremble and be sore afraid; and they will call on the rocks and mountains to cover them, and hide them from the face of the Almighty.

I call on thee O Zion, to keep my Holy laws and commandments, without the least deviation from the true spirit of the Gospel; also to walk low and humbly, and pray to Me, by night and day; for in times of my own appointing, I will send exceeding heavy sufferings upon you; that I may in truth call you my well tried and beloved few, and that you may be true examples of patience, and meekness, to all who come to learn the way of peace and righteousness.

And more than this, I do require you to be so prepared, that you can stand united in one spirit, steadfast as the rock of ages, and keep your faith firm and unshaken, although you may be called to suffer imprisonment, banishment, and many other cruel and barbarous things, which the wicked may inflict upon you.

But remember, my beloved few, if you will keep my Holy way, and cry to Me in meekness, and humiliation, with one spirit and one mind, desiring Me to help you to endure, I will not leave nor forsake you; but in all that bear for righteousness' sake, I will be with you, and my hand shall be as the strength of thousands in your defence, yea, I will watch over the lambs of my fold, and will protect my heritage, and rescue them from danger, so that not one upright soul shall be lost.

When I had written my word for the nations of the earth, I called certain of my Angels, and read it in their hearing; and they bowed and said, Amen to what thou hast written, O Lord; but who shall reveal it to mortals? for great indeed is the weight which it doth bring.

Then I chose from among the Angels, one of the most Holy, and clothed the same with my Spirit; and told him to go to the Holy Mount, where dwell my daughter's firstborn, and, as soon as he could, to show it to some of my instruments there; and according as I commanded the Angel, so was it done, and the Angel returned to Me, with the Roll, to wait for the time, that what was therein contained should be revealed.

And when the Angel returned, I was troubled, because of the heavy sufferings, and deep tribulation which I knew it would bring upon my people; both in preparing it for the nations of the earth, and from what would take place after it was spread abroad. But now my spirit rejoices, to see that my word is correctly copied; and that it is owned and blessed by my Holy Anointed, as far as it has been made known. And I do truly desire that every branch of my Holy house may lend a liberal hand in the expense of preparing my word for the nations and kindreds of the earth; and you shall not be the losers, but your reward shall be double what you give.

I do also desire that each and every one would carefully and wisely consider their present day, and calling, and labor to walk according to it. For if you are ever so faithful, you cannot be too well prepared for days to come, in which you will see much tribulation, and many heavy trials.

I have for some time past, been careful to warn all my people to prepare, for I would surely do a great work in the earth, through which no soul would be able to stand, and find favor in my sight, but such as would hearken to my warnings. And now, as the time is drawing very near, and is even at the door, I say, blessed are ye that have harkened to my warnings, and have kept my commandments; for it shall be well with you: and those who have not done this, must bear the reward of their own labor, and feast upon such fruit as they have gathered. For I have been merciful to all, and sent repeated and timely warnings ; that all who had done wrong, and wandered from the path, might have time to see their own state, repent and come down, where they could find their union and relation with Me, by obedience to the order which I have established for the protection and safe-going of my people.

Now, I say unto all who love my ways, walk in them ; Fear not the slanders of the wicked, nor the reproach of the ungodly ; for my Holy Zion, shall sit as a Queen, and feast on the good of her labors, while those who will not obey my voice, shall perish in the dust.

Great and marvellous is the work which I will do before the eyes of many who are now living; therefore I say, Prepare, and do not delay the time, for you know not the day or hour in which I will do my work, and bring to pass that which I have promised by the word of my mouth. And lest you should be like the unbelieving Jews, I say again, Prepare, O prepare ! and do not delay the time till it is too late.

This seal I give unto you, my beloved and well tried servants, as an evidence, and a warning to my people to prepare for the great day of my visitation among the nations and kingdoms of the earth ; which will deeply interest every faithful child of my holy house upon earth.

Inspired writer of the foregoing Communications,
MARY ANN JENNINGS.
Union Village, Warren County, State of Ohio.

Extracts from the testimony of Benjamin Seth Youngs.
I was born in Schenectady, State of New York, Sept. seventeenth, seventeen hundred and seventy-four.

I have been a member of the United Society called "Believers" in the present appearing of Christ, for upwards of forty-nine years. I have been, for longer and shorter periods of time, personally and intimately acquainted with all the United Societies in the United States, (except two in the State of Maine;) at New Lebanon, Watervliet and Groveland, in the State of New York; at Hancock, Tyringham, Harvard and Shirley, in the State of Massachusetts; at Enfield in the State of Connecticut; at Canterbury and Enfield, in the State of New Hampshire; at Union Village, New Lebanon; Watervliet, near Dayton; North Union, near Cleaveland, and Whitewater Village, in the State of Ohio; at Pleasant Hill, on Shawnee Run; and South Union, (Jasper Valley) in the State of Kentucky.

In the year eighteen hundred five, I was sent (on foot with two others) as a messenger to the Western country, particularly to the people of the revival in Kentucky, and the adjacent States.

After remaining in the Western country for upwards of thirty years, during which time I was employed as a public writer and speaker, and as one of the leaders, I returned with others of my brethren and sisters from the east, who had presided in different parts, until the churches and societies were in that country established.

And I do testify from indisputable evidence, and with the most scrupulous regard to truth, that the messages and communications proceeding from their mouths, were not of mortal diction, but by the Divine agency, they were uttered, and that they proceeded from the source of eternal truth, as their sacred writings also bear witness.

The foregoing Sacred Roll I have heard read before a large assembly, by the chosen mortal instrument that wrote it. I do bear witness and testify, that the contents of this Sacred Roll and book, came from, and are sent forth to mortals by God the Father, the Creator of heaven and earth.

To conclude, that great and distressing calamities, by sea and land, by fire and flood, are fast approaching, and that the mighty angels of the God of heaven, have already gone forth, to execute his judgments in the earth, there is no doubt. And from what we have seen, heard and felt, of the very wonderful works of God among his people, within the few years past, we are compelled to accord with the language of the Holy Spirit, Great and marvellous are thy works Lord God Almighty, Just and true are thy ways, thou King of Saints. Who shall not fear thee, O Lord, and glorify thy name, for thy judgments are made manifest.

With true and pure regard for the peace, prosperity and happiness of my fellow mortals, I am

BENJAMIN SETH YOUNGS.

Watervliet, Aug. 28, 1843.

Here close the extracts from the "Sacred Roll and Book." I have selected them with the intention of giving as correct an idea of the book as could be obtained without reading the whole of it. If the selections fail of being a fair sample of the book, it is because they are the most interesting portions of it. Much of the book is dull and prosy; especially the "First Part." Doubtless I have extracted as much from it as will be interesting to the reader. And the extracts give a fair idea of its character and pretensions; of the nature and quality of its inspiration.

It is entirely unnecessary to use any arguments to show the fallacy of the pretensions of this book to inspiration. None but those who are strongly bound by Shaker superstition can receive it as inspired. And they even, will reject it, as soon as they have sufficient liberty to question its pretensions. I cannot believe that the "Beloved Lead" themselves have any faith in it. It is a part of their policy used to maintain their influence and authority over the "Simple Ones." Of course this authority is exercised for the good of the governed. But I must notice one or two curiosities in these extracts from the "Second Part."

The testimony of the "Eleven Mighty Angels." Who will presume to question the testimony of angels? But how do we know that angels have spoken to us? Why; Harriet Goodwin, a young Shakeress, with a brilliant imagination, but entirely subject to her *Lead*, as obedient to them as a little child to its parents, a mere passive instrument in their hands, has assured us that the angels have spoken to us through her as an instrument. The whole of their spirit testimony is dependent on *her* human testimony. The testimony of this young woman. If her testimony is true, it is good for herself, and she has seen and conversed with the angels; otherwise the whole is false. So we perceive that her *single* testimony is worth just as much by itself alone, and is just as strong proof of the inspiration of the Roll and Book, as when joined with that of the "Eleven Angels." For if her testimony proves false, no angels have spoken to her. What she pretends they have said to her, must be received wholly on her authority. She might just as well have told us that she had the testimony of five hundred holy and mighty angels, as of eleven. It would be worth just as much and no more. The whole would be but the testimony of Harriet Goodwin. And it would not be strange, but exactly like a great multitude of cases which have happened among the Shakers, if some day, she should withdraw from the influence and authority of her "Lead," and tell us that she wrote these things "to please the elders." Or through an excited imagination.

She saw in her visions a great many angels. She saw four thousand angels, which watched over Philemon while copying the "Roll." She saw one angel on the fifth of February, which had a head like a lion. This is the only one she pretends to describe. Are we to judge from the description of this one, that the four thousand were also monsters in appearance? And also the eleven whose testimony we have copied? If so, I would seriously submit whether it is reasonable to suppose that God would send us such witnesses. There is also another angel described in the communication of Adah Zillah Potter, and I do not recollect that the inspired ones have given us a particular description of any of the inhabitants of the spiritual world save these two angels. Miss Potter's angel is described thus, "The appearance was solemn and terrible, for the body, from the neck, was like that of a mighty man, and the head was like that of an eagle. He had four exceedingly large wings, two upon each shoulder; these were open and spread each way. The feet were like the feet of an elephant, and seemed to be well shod with cast iron.

This must have been a most curious sight. Think of the eagle head. What would O. S. Fowler do with this head, viewing it phrenologically? But the study of phrenology is strictly forbidden by God in his holy laws to the Shakers. And no wonder if he sends them messengers with such heads. And look at the feet. "Like the feet of an elephant, and well shod with cast iron." But as the elephant's foot has no hoof like the ox and the horse, it must have been a great cruelty to nail on the iron shoes. A head like that of an eagle, feet like those of an elephant, a body like that of a mighty man, and four mighty pinions distended! Behold and wonder!

On a certain occasion I intimated to the Shakers that it was an objection to their revelation, that it represented the angels to be such monsters. When they referred me to the vision of John, recorded in revelations, or that part of it in the fourth Chapter, which speaks of the "four beasts" as a parallel case. But there is a very great difference in the two cases. In the first place, those described in the Shaker revelation, are represented as real angels, with a message from *God* to mortals. But those in John's revelation, are represented, not as angels, but as *Beasts*. In the second place, while the Shaker angels are set forth as real intelligences, the "beasts or living creatures" seen by John, as all commentators and theologians agree with all common sense, were but *emblems*, presented to the apostle's mind in a vision. What these emblems were designed to teach is another question, but that they were emblems there is no doubt. The writers of the Bible frequently bring such emblems to our view, but no where do they describe the angels or messengers of God as monsters.

The writer of the "Sacred Roll" inserts a note in Miss Goodwin's communication, stating in effect that she knew nothing of her statements concerning the "Sacred Roll" except through inspiration. For although these things had been revealed to him, he had kept them "entirely within himself." It would seem from some expressions in her communication that she and Philemon live in the same house. Philemon is second elder in the family; and when one of the Holy Laws forbids that the brethren should enter the sisters rooms without knocking and being bid come in; it is said in connexion, " These laws are not designed to apply to the elders!" Now does not Philemon and the rest of the Lead see on reflection, that it is much easier for the world to believe that under all the circumstances of the case, it is far more likely that he and Miss Goodwin should conspire to have a marvellous agreement in their testimonies, than that they should have a divine inspiration to write these things.

Gifts of healing.

The Shakers have made great pretentions to the power of healing miraculously. I had related to me while among them many wonderful cases. There are also many cases recorded in a published work of theirs, entitled "*Testimonies concerning the character and ministry of Mother Ann Lee.*" I never had the priveledge of witnessing any efforts of this kind while among them; but will relate here a single case, which I had from the lips of a *Subject* of miraculous healing. This miracle was notorious among the Shakers, and I had an account of it in the family where I resided, but much exaggerated and altered from what it is as I received it from the subject of it herself. The subject of this miracle was a sister of the Second family, familiarly called "Aunt Easter." As my interest in this matter had been excited by the account I had received of it, I determined to improve the first opportunity to see Aunt Easter, and criticise this miracle so far as I could without wounding her feelings by coming in conflict with her prejudices. I will here transcribe the account of my interview with her, as I recorded it immediately after returning home.

January 2d, Sabbath, 1845, was present at the funeral

of Pitman Cook, an aged brother of the 2d family. He was 87 years old, had been personally acquainted with Mother Ann. After the usual ceremonies, and while the procession moved to the grave, remaining at the house I asked and obtained leave of the eldress to have an interview with Easter Williams (aunt Easter.) I told her I heard of the miracle by which she had been healed, and wished very much to hear some account of it from herself, if she would be so kind as to favor me with it.

This gift was administered to her about twenty years ago. She had then been a cripple about nineteen years. caused by falling through a loose floor or between the joist prepared for laying a floor, upon which some loose boards had been thrown. By this fall, she injured her hips; the right hip much more than the left, and also the small of her back. I asked, did you have a physician? Yea, a very skillful physician too. What did he say of the injury? did he say it was a dislocation of the hip joint? or a fracture of any bone? or an injury of the spine? Nay; he did not call it by any name; only he said it was injured very badly. And nothing could be done for it but to keep the parts from mortifying. She was so badly crippled, that for 19 years she was unable to raise herself from her chair without assistance. When lifted up and crutches placed under her arms, she could move slowly about upon the level floor; but could not go up or down a flight of stairs. About a year after her misfortune, she had a dream or night vision, in which a heavenly Messenger appeared to her and promised her that she should be healed, but not until after a long season. Probably her injury was as great as here represented. And doubtless she had the dream also which she related.

The miraculous healing took place during the time of a remarkable revival of the faith among them. The day before the healing (Saturday, I think,) the instrument through whom the myracle was wrought, Molly Turner, came to her, and told her she felt a gift for her. Molly Turner lived in the same family with Easter, the second family; and was, they told me, a great portion of the time under the operation of the Spirit. Doubtless, Aunt Easter having all faith in these things, had her mind well prepared for the miracle. The instrument talked with her on Saturday, and the next morning, or forenoon, came and talked with her again about it; told her she must lie down, and helped her on to the bed. And while the families were assembled at the meeting-house, for their usual worship, the instrument, Molly Turner, felt a special gift for her, (Easter,) felt that she must go home and administer it to her. After the meeting was closed at the meeting-house, she came home, went to Easter, and performed manipulations over her body, especially over the parts which had been injured.

In the evening, Sunday Evening, the family held a meeting in their family dwelling as is their custom. The meeting room was adjoining the room where Easter was lying on her bed. During this meeting, Miss Turner, went to her again and exerted her miraculous powers; and, finally took hold of her, and asked her if she did not want to go into the meeting. She replied that she did. The instrument then helped her up and led her into the meeting room, without her crutches; and joined in the exercises, dancing, &c. She continued to labor thus by turns through the meeting; occasionally sitting down to rest, and getting up again without help and laboring without crutches. These things she had not been able to do before since the accident by which she received her injury. About nineteen years. And that night she walked down stairs to her supper, and back again to her chamber without help, and without her crutches. And has never used her crutches since that time, but has been able to walk without them.

Now, these statements are probably very nearly correct. They may be a little exaggerated. Why then is not this a miracle indeed? By asking her a few questions, I drew out the following facts. First, if we call this a cure, or healing, it was very imperfect. Although she actually got up and went into the meeting room as related above, she told me, it was only through the greatest exertions, and the most excruciating pain that she could do so. And although she actually went down stairs to her supper, and if I remember aright, she told me also that she went down to her breakfast the next morning. But it gave her so much pain, and fatigue, that the eldress perceiving she was not able to endure it, forbid her coming down again. And although she has not used her crutches since the miracle was wrought, she can only just hobble about over the level floor; and with much exertion, can move a few steps out of doors, where the ground is very smooth and level. This is the extent of the cure, the magnitude of the miracle.

The amount of the miracle is this. The woman was lame; her hip joints were not entirely useless as she could move about with crutches. Those joints were doubtless in a measure stiffened, or calloused. And now, when her mind was wrought up to the highest enthusiasm, believing she was about to be myraculously healed, making an extraordinary effort, she succeeded in a small degree in breaking up the old callous, or stiffness, and is just able to hobble about without her crutches. Her belief in the pretentions of Molly Turner, merely furnished the occasion for the effort which was doubtless a benefit to her. But it is clear to me that every thing about the case is perfectly natural, and easily accounted for on natural principles, and, therefore, is no miracle at all.

We may safely assume that if her healing had been by a Divine agency, it would have been perfect. The works of God are all perfect. None of the lame, or blind, or sick, healed by Christ, or his Apostles, were partially cured, but their restoration in every case, was perfect. But " Aunt Easter," is nearly as lame as she ever was.

Nevertheless this is a fair specimen of Shaker miracles, and no doubt as good a miracle as they have on record. It is much talked of and much account is made of it among them. As I heard the account of this miracle, as it was received among the brethren and sisters, she was represented as having been perfectly restored. It was said that immediately on being restored, she leaped, and shouted, ran up and down stairs, and through the halls of the house, with the fleetness and buoyancy of a girl of ten years old; and when she first bent her joints, they "snapped like a pistol." This is the version of the affair *generally* propagated for effect. The one taken from the mouth of the subject herself, is the first edition, and probably pretty correct.

Now, so long as the "Lead" in the denomination can cause the mass of the members to believe these things, the miracles, the visions, revelations, the holy laws, and orders, as coming from God: they will be able to maintain their absolute authority, and unlimited power over them. And it makes no difference whether these revelations come directly through the elders themselves, or the lay members of the order. For the prophets, and prophetesses, are but the passive instruments of their "Lead." They know very well that all their revelations must be in union with the views and feelings of the elders. Nothing is allowed to be revelation which does not have their sanction. All the laws, and orders, of the denomination, are in harmony with this fact. I have already given some specimens of these, which go to show the perfect subordination of this community to their elders. All these things are designed and calculated to maintain, and increase, the power and authority of the ministry, and elders, and procure the entire obedience and submission of the members. All preaching as well as all revelation is directed to this point. Great and continual effort is made to impress it upon every one that the salvation of his soul depends upon his obedience to the elders. "Obedience to the elders is obedience to God." It was remarked by one of the sisters in the ministry at Canterbury, while visiting our society, in discussing, or speaking of the good effects of the gift of the Father and Son, that "it had had one good effect, it made the brethren and sisters more obedient." Now, this remark, though apparently very trifling in itself, is a good expression of a sentiment which obtains with the Lead. No means are left unused which will tend to accomplish this end. The most effectual means to this end is in the confession of sins.

Confession of Sins.

This is a vital doctrine in Shakerism. It is the door of entrance to this kingdom. One is said to " set out in this way," when he opens his mind, or confesses his sins, to the elder. When he has done this, he is received as a brother. And he can have no union with them as a Christian, until he has done this.

The order of confession usually observed, is, that the brethren confess to the elder, and the sisters to the eldress. The second elder generally receives the confessions of the younger brethren of the family, and the second eldress of the young sisters. " In the first of the faith," as they express it, there were cases in which sisters opened their minds to the elders. And men confessed to Ann Lee. The Shakers do not speak of it as confessing their sins to the elders. But as " confessing them to God before his chosen witnesses."

It is one of the principal doctrines of the denomination, and is continually and strenuously inculcated, as necessary to salvation, that one should faithfully confess to the elders *all* the sins of which he has been guilty through his whole life. And they must be confessed one by one as they may occur to his mind. As they are confessed, we were taught, they are blotted out from the record on high. *Confession* and *obedience* we were taught, are the only conditions of forgiveness, and salvation. We were sometimes exhorted by the ministry, not to have any secrets of our own ; were assured, the elders were our best friends, and we should unfold all our secrets to them. Our safety and happiness, we were told, depended upon our doing so.

Every one is required upon entering the community to unfold his mind to the elder without reserve. And then, many times in the course of the year, on every important occasion, the brethren and sisters, are severally called upon to unburden their minds to the elders; as on " Fast Day," also, before receiving any important gift, as the cleansing gift, the gift of the Father and Son, also before meeting on the mountain, &c. Also, it is required of every one, if he commit any sin, that he should not go into meeting, until it is confessed. It is expected of the young sisters that they go to confession, as often at least, as two or three times a week. Any violation of any of the laws, and orders of the denomination is pronounced by Divine authority to be sin, and must be confessed. It is a sin for a brother to shake hands with, or touch a woman, whether a world's woman, or a " believer." It is a sin to sit cross-leged in union meeting; as we stand in our meetings for worship, it is a sin not to fold the hands with the right thumb over the left; when we retire to rest, it is a sin not to lay straight and take our rest in the fear of God. The laws, and orders, of this kind are greatly multiplied, and it is declared that the breaking of the least of these is a sin. So that confessions are very frequent; probably not a day passes but the elders hear more or less of them. The true and faithful " believers," unfold to their elders, the whole heart without reserve.

The elders faithfully report these confessions to the ministry of their society; and the ministry report faithfully to the Pontiff at the head of influence, at New Lebanon. By this means, not only is the condition and character of every member known, but likewise his passions and propensities. This is the secret lever by which the Shaker despotism has been wielded so long and so successfully. The elders are intimately acquainted with the thoughts and feelings, purposes and propensities, character and condition of the several members of the several families of the denomination. And consequently know exactly what influences to exert to keep them in subjection. And the elders are politic in the management of their subjects. They are more lenient with young believers or new comers than with the old, and grant them many more privileges; and teach them doctrines and duties as they are able to receive them. As they often express themselves, the Shaker life is a *travel*. Every one is expected to make some " travel in the gospel." The gospel is imparted to them as they are able to bear it. Some families have revelations or gifts which other families are not sufficiently advanced to receive. Some families are subject to some laws and orders, which are not enforced upon other families. Speaking after the manner of Paul, the babes are fed with milk, and men with strong meat. And the ministry learning the spiritual condition and wants of the several families from the elders, know what rules and orders to make for them. And the ministry at the head of influence learning from the subordinate ministry the condition and wants of the various societies and families, conduct the government accordingly.

But there are often some who by reason of infidelity of belief, or from some motive, do not faithfully confess their sins; have secrets they do not choose to entrust with the elder. But the delinquency of such is soon detected by the elder. But the very fact that he does not confess faithfully is proof that his faith is waiving, and that he is in the way of disobedience. The Shaker inquisition is brought to bear upon him. For it must be borne in mind that every true Shaker, every one who loves that "way and work," feels as much a duty in informing the elders of any disobedience, or infidelity in a brother or sister, as in confessing his own sins. And by so doing he not only assists to restore that brother or sister to the path of duty and the way of life, but also gains favor with the elders. So that duty and interest combine to bring to light every hidden sin, and every secret among the brethren and sisters.

It is nothing against the character of a Shaker, but rather meritorious to be a listener and an informer. The elders are very faithful not to expose an informer to those informed against. All heavy walking or loud talking in the halls of the house, is strictly forbidden. And it is alledged as a reason, that such things displease the invisible Spirits which are constantly present. This affords an excuse for listeners to be near in a sly and unexpected manner; suddenly appear in the rooms of others without any warning; and thus use all the means of detection without seeming to design it.

It is also strictly against "holy order," for any brother

or sister to keep any thing under lock and key. ("This law does not apply to the elders.") If therefore any thing is found locked up without the direction or permission of the elders, it is against order, and it is the duty of the elders to look into the matter. I have just received a letter from an acquaintance who still resides in the family where we resided, and with whom I have had considerable correspondence, in which he informs me that with false keys, they have opened his trunk and read our correspondence. There must be, and there can be no secrets from the elders.

The Shakers maintain just as thorough an inquisition as ever the catholics did in Spain or at Rome; though none of their physical tortures, to enforce their commands. For this reason, it has always been impossible to form any extensive combination against the government, or the authority of the Lead. It is strictly against order for any one to express any doubts or unbelief of any thing pertaining to Shakerism, to any except the elders or those who are well established in the faith. If one presumes to do so, and continues in such a course, the brethren and sisters are warned against such a one, and not unfrequently forbidden to associate with him; and he is hurried away into the world as soon as possible, unless there is good hope of repentance.

Whenever one becomes unmanageable and disobedient, measures are taken to get rid of him. Doubtless if all who have withdrawn from this denomination, could be numbered, they would considerably exceed those who remain in the denomination. But not being able to combine together while in the denomination, they were easily ejected one by one, by the united strength of this people. And having departed from the society, they no longer have any claim upon it, according to their covenant obligations.

Probably very few of the members except the lead, understand the object, or use made of their confessions. They are taught that *God requires* that every thing should be confessed to the elders. And when a sin is confessed, it is forgiven. This is the extent of their knowledge, and the end of their concern in the matter. One day while I was with that people, observing the elders just moving away towards the ministry's shops, for it is in their work shops only that they receive the elders, (their dwelling in upper story of the meeting house being too sacred for any to enter but themselves, unless it be on some very extra occasion ;) this was on or after a general confession in the family, I asked some of the young brethren why it was, that the elders invariably visited the ministry directly after a day of confession? They very seldom went there all together on any other occasion. After a moment's thought they recollected that this had generally if not always been the case. And now for the first time, it occurred to them that it might be to report the confessions of the members of the family.

When I went before the elder for the purpose of confession, he expressed himself to me very nearly in the following language. "Now David, you need not fear to unfold any thing to me which comes to your mind, for we are solemnly pledged that nothing which is opened, (that is confessed) to us shall go any farther." At the time I took him to mean strictly what he said. And that the elders never related to any human being. And the brethren with whom I conversed on the subject, said that the elders felt it a duty not to call to their own minds even, confessions which had been made. Probably the elder meant by his remark to me, "We are solemnly pledged," that is the ministry and elders are thus pledged, that confessions shall "go no farther," that is, shall not go beyond the ministry and elders.

The real fact in the case is this. The elders and eldresses of the family, meet together and talk over familiarly the confessions which are made to them ; and report them faithfully to the ministry. The two elders and eldresses of the family hold three meetings in every week, in the private apartments of the elders, at which they have ample opportunity to talk over such matters.

Sometimes some curious and extravagant confessions

come to the ears of some of the brethren and sisters who are in the confidence of the elders. Some such confessions came to my knowledge, but are of such a character as not to be suitable for this publication. They are of such a nature as to show beyond doubt, that things confessed to the eldresses, also come to the knowledge of the elders. And things revealed to the elders, come to the knowledge of the eldresses. Things of a very indelicate nature.

But this knowledge is necessary that the ministry and elders may know how to combine and direct their influence for the government of the whole.

This community of property also enlarges and perpetuates the power and authority of the Lead. The whole property is under the control of the ministry and elders. The trustees and all other officers are appointed by them, and serve during their pleasure. All appropriations and purchases of consequence must have their sanction to be of validity. No individual is allowed to have any thing he can call his own. Not even the clothes he wears. For often when a sister " turns off," the best portions of her clothing are retained without her consent. Formerly, the younger brethren were allowed by extra work or other innocent means, to obtain a little money for their own use. But a few years ago there came an order strictly forbiding this indulgence, and requiring all who had made any such little savings, should at once resign them to the elders. There is no privilege or opportunity for the common members to spend money. They are required and expected to remain at home and work for the good of the community, under the direction of their elders. And in this condition all the actual wants of the body are amply provided for by those who have the care of such matters.

The members are solemnly bound by the Shaker covenant which they sign on becoming of age, not to take or claim any thing to carry away with them if they ever withdraw from the community. And resign pretty much all other rights. What I say in relation to this instrument, must be from what I have been told concerning it, and from inferences drawn from known facts, never having the privilege of seeing it. Soon after going among this people I asked the privilege of seeing their covenant. But the elders doubtless knowing that I could not then sign that instrument, thought it good policy not to let me see it; lest it should seem to me too great an obstacle to surmount in becoming a Shaker. I did not "*travel*" far enough in two years to be able to bear the sight of this covenant. Others also were refused a sight of it. But it is a notorious fact, that those covenant members who leave the Shakers can never by law obtain any wages for labor performed, or any portion of the community property. Those who have carried property there and consecrated it by signing the covenant, can never reclaim it by process of law. At least this never has been done. So that in reality the lay members of the community are entirely at the disposal of their Lead. They may remain there and render implicit obedience to all their requirements, both reasonable and unreasonable, foolish and wise; " must be as obedient to the elders as little children are to their parents," or be turned out into the wicked world, exposed penniless to all its temptations and hardships. If he remain, the ministry and elders presume to take possession, not only of his property, and the proceeds of his labor, but also of all his secrets, all his thoughts and all his affections. (for no Shaker may exercise any natural affections, but must crucify them all; this is his first duty,) of his intellect and soul. No brother or sister is allowed to read any books or papers, but those printed by "believers," or recommended by the elders. It it is their policy, and is essential to their power and authority, to keep the community as ignorant as possible. He must bow down to all their superstitions, and all their pretended revelations, visions, dreams, and the fulminations of perverted imaginations of those whom the elders are disposed to use as instruments to promote their ambitious aims for power and dominion. These form the links of the chain by which every lay member is bound in Shaker bondage.

What though it be said they remain there voluntarily?

So it is said also of the southern slave; he will not leave his master and chains. Poor thing! his soul is crushed; he does not perceive that he is a man; he knows not the rights of his being; he cannot appreciate the blessings of liberty. Too much "larnin," too much knowledge would ruin him for his master. He surely would "turn off." I would by no means imply here that any class of people in these free states, are as degraded as the southern slaves. Far from it. The slaves are degraded by vice as well as ignorance. It is the system of Shakerism of which I speak. It can never have its full and legitimate effect upon its subjects, in these free states. It is surrounded by too many counteracting influences. But when carried out fully, according to its laws and orders, and it is carried to a great extent secretly even here, it makes its subjects as really slaves as are those at the South. Superstition is more efficient over a large portion of the members here, than is the driver's whip at the South. Their toil is as unrequited as that of the slave; and like him they can call nothing their own. Their submission to the elders, is required to be just as entire as that of the slave to his master.

Shakerism is therefore nothing more nor less than a system of slavery, carried on by cunning and fraud. A game perpetrated upon the innocent and unsuspecting by the crafty. It seems to me that the preceding facts developed by the system, when carefully considered, show how the game is managed. By means of a covenant, by which every thing is consecrated and placed unreservedly in the hands of the Lead. Those who do not sign the covenant, sign a written and sealed agreement to work for their board and clothing. I have now the instrument which I signed with them. The property is deeded to the trustees and their successors in office, forever, instead of, to their heirs and assigns.

By means of a covenant and agreements, confessions and humiliations, mysteries and revelations, holy laws and orders, inquisitions and espionage, preaching, exhortation and argument, the love of home and of friends, by taking away the key of knowledge, by kindness, by love, by excitement and the power of animal magnetism, and by all other means in their power, the ministry and elders are diligent in using to keep their subjects in perfect subjection; and make them useful in promoting the interest and increasing the wealth of the denomination.

And notwithstanding all these exertions, the many new and stringent measures practiced now which were not practiced formerly, yet Shakerism is manifestly on the wane. The proportionate number who leave them every year, is perpetually increasing. And of the numbers who join them, few indeed are those who stay for any considerable length of time. Judging of other societies by the one where we were, the denomination has been reduced one half within less than twenty years. Great pains are taken to keep this fact from the knowledge of common members. When the ministry spoke of the languishing condition of our society, they represented other societies as flourishing. Our minister, elder Nathaniel Deming, assured us that there was a "host of young men at New Lebanon." But those who have left that society do not represent that a very great host is left behind.

The common members are not allowed to visit from one society to another as formerly, probably it is not safe for them to have so free intercourse, nor well that they should know the condition of the denomination. There was fear expressed in our society, that enough young people would not remain to take care of and make the aged comfortable through life. And they had reason to fear this. Many have left since, and very few remain. It is evident to me that Shakerism cannot hold out much longer. Perhaps not more than twenty years. Certainly not forty. Probably some who were cotemporary with its founder, Ann Lee, will live to see it nearly to the end. They already behold it waning rapidly. Elder Nathaniel used to say, " if you turn off so that there is only four of us left, we shall constitute the society and shall hold on."

It is an interesting question, what will become of their immense property when the dissolution comes? for come it will, and come it must. There will be some who will scramble in opposition to the ministry and elders. I think covenant members would do well to hold on. I have a plan for those who get their eyes open to the fraud of Shakerism.

The covenant, although it may be of legal force, is not *morally* binding on the members. If a promise be obtained through deception or fear, it has no moral force on the promiser. If a person, in order to save his natural life, or his immortal soul, be deluded into a false oath, the obligation of such oath passes away with the delusion.

For example, if a man be seized by a band of murderers or pirates, and forced to take their oath and become one of them; he is morally bound, notwithstanding his oath, to leave them on the first opportunity; and instead of assisting them to murder for booty or any other purpose, he is bound to protect the innocent and save life.

The Thugs of India, murder from religious principle, but they are bound by all righteous considerations to abandon the practice as soon as their delusion is dispelled.

I design no disparagement to the Shakers by these comparisons. But they are to the point. The Shaker covenant is the bond of a fraudulent agreement, a means of obtaining goods by false pretences. The subjects are compelled to subscribe it by false fears excited by superstition. They are imposed on by the ministry and elders, who have a knowledge of the facts and consequences of the whole case.

They are brought under the influence of this delusion, and these fears by the exertions of the ministry and elders, and by this means compelled to take an oath to do a wrong action, viz. to support the " Lead " in practicing this fraud upon themselves and others. When therefore their eyes are opened and the delusion passes away, he is as truly bound to forsake the wrong, and counteract the mischiefs of his error, as is the pirate, or the " Thug." If the religion be false the covenant is wrong. And every true man is bound to seek its overthrow.

Let them not leave their home. I am perfectly aware

that the ministry, and elders, have always made the brethren and sisters believe that they have power to drive off the disobedient. But if they do not violate their covenant, and are forced to leave, they can recover by process of law, perhaps not wages, but an equal portion of all the property held by the society, to which they belonged. I have been told that the Shakers have had some sad experience by reason of driving away covenant members.

Then do not withdraw; do not forake your home; but insist upon getting your victuals, and clothes, where you have done your work, and enter into correspondence with those who are similarly situated with yourself. Form a party, it is easier to overturn this kingdom than you imagine. All that is wanting is a rallying point, or head. If there was one established, if they could have any confidence of success, many would join it at once. Let every one maintain as much union, as he can with his elders and the society, and maintain the doctrine that they have no authority to turn away any brother, or sister. Also, that every one has a right to an equal portion of the property, held by the society, and is under no obligations to believe all the incredible things which the elders require. Maintain these points, insist upon your rights, and seek a free intercourse with your brethren; and circumstances will teach you what to do. Your party will increase and light will break in.

Management of Children.

Having shown how the Leaders obtain, and maintain their power, and influence over the Lay members; it is proper to give some examples of their use of this power. I have already remarked upon their system of education. So far as I know, the children are well clothed, well fed, and well lodged; and not required to work beyond their strength. They are of course clothed in the Shaker garb, which is coarse and odd, and gives them an uninteresting and uninviting appearance. Much pains are taken to prejudice them against the wicked world; and to instill in their minds all their own superstitions and peculiar notions. All is peculiarly adapted to unfit them for any other society. There are indeed some very strong objections to their management of children.

In the first place no amusements, or recreations, are allowed them. This is the principle they adopt. There are some exceptions. In the church family they took in about thirty children, about the year 1844. The half of these at least were boys. The first winter they were allowed to have each a little sled, and to play upon the hardened snow. And perhaps some other recreations. It was doubtless thought too great a change, as they had just come in from the world, to break off all amusements at once. The doctrine, or principle, was well expressed by David Terry, one their preachers, and having the care of the West Family, in Hancock. He had been to Enfield on a visit; and it was at the meeting-house, on Sunday. He said the children there had given up all their plays; it was found to be just as well for them to have some useful employment. Work answered every purpose of play. They had not been seen to slide down hill this winter, nor snow ball. This is probably the sentiment of the denomination. And it was the practice so far as my observation extended.

Now, it appears to me that the exhiliration of spirits which the various simple amusements to which children are inclined, afford, is necessary, if not to health, yet to the full developement of the mind. Especially is this the case with females who do not labor in the open air. Play is so natural to children, that for them to be confined to one routine of duty and labor, perpetually guarded from relaxation by an overseer, must inevitably stint the mind in its naural developements, and energies. And also, I believe it must be a great injury to the physical system. It is both injurious, and cruel, to keep children thus confined for no crime, and thus deprive them of their natural enjoyments. It is a kind of States-Prison life; a species of slavery. But it crushes and stints all their powers, and faculties, and thus prepares them for the slavery for which they are designed.

A brother is appointed to the care of the boys, and it is his business to direct their education, employment, and all their outgoings, and incomings. If they have relatives in the world who visit them, he must be with them and watch the conversation, and see that they are not enticed away. A sister is also appointed to the same office, and duties, with the girls. The boys and girls not only are guarded in this way, but also the young men and women. Two of the young sisters in our family were visited by their mother while we were there. The age of these sisters, the youngest I think, was 17, the other 25. The second eldress who had the care of them, did not allow to see their own natural mother except in her presence. I remember another case like this. One of the young sisters was informed that a natural sister had called to see her at the office where all visiters are received. She seemed agitated, and went after the second eldress; and they two prepared themselves by adjusting their attire, and went together to meet the sister. Now, this young woman could not be permitted to see this, her own natural sister alone, lest her mind should be corrupted, and she led away to the world. I give these as fair specimens of the general practice. They go to show the slavery of the system.

The elders say in reference to these things, "We don't educate our children for the world; we educate them to stay here." And so it is in fact. For although most of the children which they bring up, leave them on coming to their seniority, yet they are peculiarly unfitted by their education, and manners, to withstand the temptations, and meet the competitions of the world. They know not how to assume any care, or responsibility even for themselves. They have been clothed, and fed, and their labors directed by others. They are educated for the slavery of Shakerism. Those who put children to the Shakers ought to understand this. Although they are guarded while there from many of the vices of the world, they are far more liable to fall a sacrifice to them when they are afterwards exposed to them. They are like caged birds while there, and when they break loose from their prison, they are not at all fortified against the wiles of the destroyer. Let children be brought up any where else rather than in Shakerdom.

Robert Jenkins, a very respectable, and good, but poor man went and joined the Shakers at the City of Peace, (their village, in Hancock,) with his family, a wife and five children, two girls and three boys. They joined the Shakers some time in the year 1842. I went with my family in the spring of 1843, April. Being new comers, or as they express it, "young believers" together, we were on very friendly not to say intimate terms, while we remained there. Our intercourse was more liberal, and free than is allowable by the rules of the society, but this was winked at by the Lead on account of our infancy in the Shaker life.

But brother Robert, and sister Rhoda, (his wife,) from their faith in the Ism, and confidence in the goodness of the people, had made up their minds never to leave them. And some time in 1843, was induced to let his children go to the church family, except the eldest daughter, a girl about ten or eleven years old; who still remained in the same family with her father and mother, but was given up to the care of others. The mother at this time was in feeble health; this was one reason for giving up the children. It is the wish of the Lead that those who bring children there, should give them up, to go the church family, where the children of the society, are generally collected. And it is one condition of their reception there, that they be bound, or indentured. Brother Robert was required to give the usual bonds. I saw these writings; and recollect that the indentures were so framed as to make it obligatory on R. Jenkins, not to claim his children, or make any demands for wages, until their minority had expired. But the Shakers could return these children upon their father at any time, if they the children did not do well. So it was a one-sided agreement. I mentioned this unfairness in the agreement to Jenkins; he had observed it, and mentioned it to them. And objected that if he should alter his mind and leave this people, he could not get his children for this agreement. But they could return his children upon him at any time. But the elder assured him that there would be no trouble of that sort; if he ever wanted to take his children away, he could have them. And from this assurance he signed the obligation. But not many months after this agreement was consummated, Robert began to get his eyes open to the iniquities of the system, and to talk of withdrawing. He opened his mind to the elder on this subject.

Directly after this, his little daughter Pamelia, about ten years old, who had not been bound with the other children, but remained in this family, under the management and tuition of sisters Nancy Riley, (the second eldress,) and Sarah Smith; having been well prepared by the skill and cunning of her keepers, came to her father, and throwing herself on her knees before him, besought him in the most pathetic and eloquent manner, the tears flooding her face, to promise her that if he left the people, he would not take her away. Her feelings were wrought up to that extent, which produced illness and vomiting. And all this was brought about by the deceitful arts of those who had the care of her, by filling her mind with their superstitions and false prejudices. I have no doubt that Jenkins is a very affectionate, kind and indulgent father. I know he has a very frank and generous disposition. Here was a severe trial to his feelings. He and his wife withdrew, and left this girl; but have since taken her away. I will give shortly an extract of a letter from him showing the manner of his getting her away.

When R. Jenkins began to think of leaving the Shakers, a very important question with him was, whether he could have his children. But the united and decisive answer of the Lead was "nay." Robert shall not have his children. So he and his "woman" (as the Shakers express it) were compelled to leave their only treasure, their children, behind. This is one of the peculiarities of Shakerism; it is not satisfied with any half way work, the whole must be sacrificed; property, children, liberty, and all the natural affections. As in the case of the man of "Luz." "Skin for skin, yea, all that a man hath will he give for his life."

But after going away and establishing himself in business, he began to devise ways and means of getting out of the Shaker bondage. On the 25th of May, 1845, he wrote thus. " On the 8th inst., I made the Shakers a visit, long to be remembered by them and me. Our school commenced, and we thought we would make the trial with Pamelia, and send her to school this summer. So we have got her from the Shakers. I assure you I had a time of it. I went over about sundown, and told elder William my errand. He thought I was not taking the wisest course * * * He went out, " but soon returned with Hannah, (the first deaconess,) Nancy, and Pamelia. Then was death in the pot. They came in with a look, and air, as much as to say, We don't care for you; you can't get P———. I soon made my errand known to Pamelia; but she refused to go with me; said she should not. And then she looked up to Nancy, and then she down on her knees, and went on the terriblest that ever was. If she had been pleading for her life, she could not have done it more earnestly. I dallied with her awhile to show her my reasons, but with no effect, until I told her to get a cloak, for she *must* go. But Nancy refused to get her something to wear, said she never should. Elder William told them to get her something to wear, and Hannah went and got her an old cloak, and then sent P——— to get her stockings on. Nancy said I would rue that nights job. I told her if I did, P——— should not be under her tuition any longer; for all the girls that she had brought up, would curse her as long as she lived. And she boiled slick over.——— P——— was homesick three or four days, but has got over it now, goes to school every day and is as lively as a kitten, and says nothing about going back."

Friend Jenkins then endeavored to persuade them to give up his children, but they steadily refused. They could not in *conscience*, give up the children, to go into the wicked world, while they were contented. But finally agreed, to compromise with him, and give them for the sum of one hundred dollars. This it would seem, being the real value of their conscience. But Jenkins being poor, could illy afford to pay this amount; but afterwards offered to give them fifty dollars for his own children. The answer was, " nay." He then requested to see his children alone, so that he could examine them without their being under the restraint of their keepers; to know if they were contented, but they utterly refused him this privilege. They assured him the children were contented, and so long as they were contented, they should keep them. This was a great affliction to the parents. Robert wrote me of this trouble, and says, "what I shall do, I know not." This was about a year after they left. He finally concluded to make some effort to get his oldest boy, when he was fourteen years of age, and he was near that age. He writes me in the same letter, " I forgot to tell you about my going to the church office the other day, to see the boys. I was on the step stone, and Lewis (his second boy, about ten years old) came round the corner of the office. As soon as he saw me, he started and run as fast as he could, till he got out of sight. So you see how they are trained to it." I am a father, and I feel that a parental affection is not to be trifled with. 'I fear I should not have borne this treatment with that christian meekness which I ought always to possess.

I cannot but feel to justify the course he has since pursued to obtain his children. I understand he has now got them all but one. Lewis is there yet.—Feb. 22d, 1846, he wrote me as follows.

We had a little brush with the Shakers, the last day of January. I went there in the evening, with six of my friends. We went into the room where the boys were. I was to take Edwin, (the oldest, about 14 years of age) my brother was to take one, and our nephew the other of the two besides. I went first into the room; went directly to Edwin, and put my hand upon his shoulder, not thinking that he would make any resistance. But he tried to get away as hard as he could. This stirred up the rest, so that they could not pick out the other boys. Consequently we got none but Edwin. He was very much frightened. We went to my father's that night, in the state of New

York, where Edwin has remained ever since. He has been well pleased and contented. This was accomplished on Saturday. On Monday morning, as I was at work as usual, the Shakers being on the wing bright and early, to know if I was in town. In the afternoon their Lawyer, P. L. Hall, came out to see me, and advised me to give up the boy, and have no more trouble about it. Told me it was a high offence, and I had better do so than let the law have its course.

"I heard him through, and then told him, that I did not fear the Shakers; they had wronged me out of my children, and now they might do their worst. The next morning Simon, (one of the deacons of the church family, and in the great gift of the Father and Son, was the incarnation of the Savior,) with the sheriff and lawyer, went to my father's to get the boy; but he want there. Simon threatened very hard, and said that neither myself or any of my friends should ever see the rest of my children, unless they gave up Edwin. But his threats amounted to nothing. They finally made Simon promise, not to take the boy back, unless he wanted to go, and on that condition consented to let him see the boy. So all hands went about three miles, to my sister's, where he was. As it happened, my brother and the lawyer got to the house first, and they told Edwin that he need not go back, unless he was a mind to, and to stick to his determination not to go back; yes, said the lawyer, yes, *stick*. My brother-in-law was with Simon, and they were bothered to find the door; (purposely I presume) however he got in, and tried to persuade Edwin to go back, but all in vain. The boy had very much changed his opinion of his friends. He told the boy, if he would return with him, and did not wish to remain, his grandfather might come the next day and take him away again. Edwin replied that he should not go. So Simon had to return without him.

I heard the same week that Lewis said, he wished his father had got him. So on Saturday, I went to see them again, but they said it was not so. I wanted to see him alone, but they would not let me. I told them they dare not. Last week I went again to get Edwin's clothes, but they would do nothing about it. So, how we shall manage to get the rest of my boys, I know not.—They have threatened me some. I tell them, if it was not for leaving my work, I had rather they would do their worst. My friends are ready to go with me and take the others by force, but that should be the last resort. The Shakers have a fine time preaching persecution."

At this time Jenkins was employed in a woollen manufactory, within about a mile of the Shaker village. After the affair of getting his oldest boy from them, the elders went directly to his employers, and complaining of the trouble he gave them, required his dismissal. So they informed him, that when the time for which he had been engaged, was expired, they could not hire him longer. And this time was near at hand. But Jenkins saw the elders, and convinced them that it would be for their interest to let him remain. So finally by their consent, he was employed another year.

I mention this, to show the influence, which the Shakers have over their neighbors. Who say of them, "the Shakers are good friends, but bad enemies." However honest and upright therefore, their neighbors may be, it is for their interest to testify in their favor.

Under date of August 21st, 1847,—He wrote me as follows. " We left the factory near the Shakers, and came to this place, Lee, for the purpose of getting our children from the Shakers. I have made two trials on them with good success. Now for the way I got them. On the afternoon of the 20th of June, we went to the Shakers, with the intention of getting Harriet, (his youngest child) if there was a chance. We got there about two o'clock, P. M. I had previously engaged a team to go to the Shaker village, and get there one hour after we did; they were to drive to the west part of the village, and when they came back, I was to put her into their waggon. For I feared the Shakers would be too much for me, if I undertook to carry her away myself alone. Edwin and Pamelia went with me.

I told Sylvia (probably one of the sisters who had the

care of the office) that we had come to see the children; and desired her to bring them as soon as she could, for there was an appearance of a shower. So she went for them, and in a short time, some of the sisters returned with Harriet only, the boys not being quite ready. There were no men present. I asked how soon the boys would be there. She said, in a short time. I thought now is my chance. I told Edwin to unhitch the horse, and by the time this was done, Pamelia, Harriet, and myself were in the waggon, and were off just as Jo. Wicker got there with the boys, and before the other team got there.

" My next game on them, was last Friday. By chance I came on the Shaker boys a short distance east of the Shaker village depot. I was about a half a mile from them when I first saw them. They were going towards the depot. Then I thought I would have a little scrape with them, my boys were eight or ten rods ahead of the rest, running as hard as they could, to get away from me. I soon overtook one of them, and started for Pittsfield with him. Went part of the way on foot, and then engaged a team to carry us the rest of the way.

" The Shakers have not made any fuss about this matter yet, except to enter a complaint to the society of Odd Fellows, of which I am a member. Here is a copy of their petition or protest."

" On the night of the 31st of January, 1846, the said Jenkins, came in a riotous manner, with a gang of ruffians, and feloniously entered a dwelling house, putting the inmates in fear, and kidnapped his oldest son.

" His next overt act in this line, was on the afternoon of the 26th of June, 1847. On that day he came to the Trustee's Office, and requested to see his children, who still remained here, viz : two sons and a daughter. The daughter was taken to see him, by the female who had the care of her, and the said Jenkins, seeing no others present, forcibly kidnapped the daughter, and ran away with her also, contrary to his agreement, and without sufficient honesty to pay for her keeping.

"The above statements can be abundantly proved, and are respectfully submitted to the lodge.
" JOSEPH PATTEN."
" We the undersigned, aver that the above statement by Joseph Patten, is correct."
" JOSEPH WICKER."
" SIMON MAYBEE."
" DAVID WOLLISON."

This really is very terrible! A father has kidnapped his own children, to deliver them from Shaker bondage, because he could get them in no other way. It is like an abolitionist, assisting the slaves of the South to their freedom. This is called, by the Slaveholders, " negro stealing," and is treated accordingly. But in fact, it is an act of christian benevolence. But this is one of the characteristics of the wicked; " they put good for evil, and evil for good. Darkness for light, and light for darkness." —I have no doubt the society of Odd Fellows, will treat this Shaker document with merited contempt.

Those who would put their children to the Shakers, should understand, that it is an important object of the Shakers, as soon as possible, to prejudice their children against the world ; and especially against their parents, if they belong to the world. It is one of their fundamental doctrines, *that all the natural affections should be crucified.* And by this they mean to include filial and parental affection.—Who can possess absolute power and not abuse it?

The way they treat those in their power who refuse obedience to the Lead.

On this subject, I will give a single specimen, which will show how they use their power. Jane Ann Weed, left the Shakers in the winter of 1845, or rather, was forcibly carried off by the Shakers for disobedience. I saw her the next March, and received from her, a particular history of her removal. And have since received her permission to publish it. She has since, also, written me an account of her going to the Shakers. Her parents had a large family of children, and were poor. She was living from home and was contented, having as she expressed it, a good place. Her parents went to the Shakers, taking all their children except this girl. They were so much pleased with the people, that they were anxious she also should come. Two Shaker brethren were sent for her. One of these was Joseph Patten, a member of the church family. The Weed family went to the gathering order, or East family. J. Ann, having a good place hesitated to go with these men. They assured her, if she did not wish to stay, they would bring her safely back again. And made her many other fair promises; by which she was finally induced to go with them. She expected to live in the same family with her parents, brothers and sisters; but when she found her mistake, she claimed her right to be returned from from whence she came, but in vain; she reminded Joseph Patten of his promise; but all did not avail her. So she was obliged to make the best she could of it. She was a prisoner, and there was no escape. And so she says, " I tried to content myself as well as I could. And did become tolerably well contented, and very much attached to my young companions. I remained there seven years. (She was between eighteen and nineteen years of age when she left the Shakers.) My attachment to my young companions, was the origin of the difficulty, which resulted in my departure from the Shakers.

For some trivial offence, my most intimate companion and myself were strictly forbidden to speak together. This companion was a Shaker sister, about my own age. This order we did not strictly observe, but sought secret interviews. But those who had the care of us, ascertained by inquisition, that our faith was wavering, and our obedience was not a full and willing obedience. My companion was soon sent off to the world. She had a great dread of the world, but all her promises, entreaties, confessions, and humiliations would not avail. She was driven off to the world without mercy. " She undoubtedly finds the world less terrible than she had been taught. But my time had not yet come. A few weeks after this, Jane Ann was also sent away. I do not recollect the immediate cause of their sending her away. It was some small matter, if any thing in particular, which offended sister Dana of the ministry.—It is to be borne in mind, that this young woman had imbibed all the Shaker prejudices against the world. Also, had no relatives or friends in the world, on whom she could depend. Although her parents had left, she could not look to them. Her father, if alive, was, where, she knew not. Her mother was in Boston, but was represented by the Shakers as a vile woman. Where then could she go? She had been notified that she must leave. She had made unreserved confessions at the time her companion left, and obtained liberty to remain. But her time had come. It was doubtless thought necessary to the safety of the young members of the family, to sacrifice her. Accordingly, the day before she was carried away, she was told to prepare to depart. She was not permitted, after receiving this notice, to speak to any of her young companions. But was taken to the Trustees' office, where strangers and worldlings are received, and locked into one of the chambers, and remained thus imprisoned through the night. Early the next morning, the second eldress of the church family went to her, and by encouraging her that she might yet be restored to union in the family, obtained her last secret, if she had any at this time. But directly, sister Dana, of the ministry came up, and knocked at the door, peremptorily demanded admittance, and vehemently forbidding the interview of the second eldress with her, at the same time, saying emphatically that *Jane Amn was not going to stay ;* but *should go.*— And poor J. Ann had such a horror of going, as made her quite ill. She was unable to eat a mouthful of breakfast. But the word had gone from sister Dana, and could not return to her void. So they gave poor Ann some kind of cordial, which enabled her to raise her head, and get into the carriage which was to convey her away. But where was the poor girl to go?

She desired to be left at Pittsfield town, thinking she could find some anti Shakers there, who would sympathise with her, and assist her in getting employment. But the decided answer was, "*nay;* you must go to Boston, where your mother is." No entreaties could alter this decision. She had two sisters at the East family. The Shakers feared greatly that she would communicate with them, and other young people in the society, and draw them away. They (the Shakers) have a great dread of anti Shakers in Pittsfield. This girl had been so accustomed to the exercise of unlimited power, that she did not even conceive the idea of resisting their authority in any other way than by begging the *privilege* of being left at Pittsfield. But when she found this poor privilege denied her, she had one more humble request to make. Her sisters in the East family knew *where* in the city, their mother was located, but *she* did not. Her request now was, that she might call at the East family, and obtain directions from her sisters, by which she could find her mother in the city. But as incredible as it may seem, this request even, was denied her. This denial, however, was *not* I think, *purely* malicious, not purely to torment this helpless and innocent girl. If she had stopped to see her sisters, the meeting might have been disastrous to *their* Shakerism, to say the least of it. I can think of no other reason

In this state of despair and ill health, this devoted young woman, eighteen years of age, who had been a caged bird for seven years, consequently knew little or nothing of the customs and manners of the world, was taken into the waggon by Joseph Wicker to be conveyed away. Joseph Wicker is the second elder of the church family; and was the incarnation of the Father, at the great gift of the Father and Son. They start away in the morning, so as to take the cars on the Western rail road for Boston. They pass hastily by the house where her sisters lived, but those sisters saw and recognized them. There is a depot in the Shaker village, but they did not stop there. They passed through Pittsfield, very near the depot, but that was not the place to take the cars. He carried her on to Dalton, and put her on board the SECOND CLASS CARS, and paid fare to Boston, accordingly. Shame! Shame! But this is not all. This girl did not go away pennyless. He put money into her hand; behold! she is going to a strange city, nearly one hundred and fifty miles from home, her passage is paid in the second class cars, and she has put into her hand! *one dollar and fifty cents!* all told.

I received this fact from her own mouth shortly after she left the people. And indeed the whole history of the case. She also wrote me afterwards, by request, and says, concerning the money, "I understand the Shakers have reported that they gave me much more money than was necessary to pay my expenses back from Boston. But this was *false, no mistake.* All the money the Shakers gave me, when they put me on board the cars, was one dollar and fifty cents."

It will be asked why they did not put her on board the cars at the nearest depot. I can think of but one reason. They were afraid she would stop at Pittsfield. Joseph saw her into the car, and stood by until the cars moved off. He then returned home, and as he passed by the East family, J. Ann's sisters, who had been watching for him, run out to hail him and inquire where he had carried their sister. He saw them coming towards him, and whipped up his horses, and shook his head at them; saying, I can't stop.

Let us again mentally return to the cars, and follow this young woman to Boston. It is well known, that this class of cars are occupied, with the exception of some business *men*, who go in them for economy's sake, by very rough people. And I cannot but regard it as a shameful economy in the Shakers, to place this young female here, to travel so far, without any protector; and in her state of health. Her grief and terror found expression in perpetual tears, which she could not restrain. There was only one woman beside herself on board this car, and she of rather a coarse and repulsive appearance. Nevertheless, J. Ann, in her extremity, appealed to her for advice and protection. The stranger very coolly referred her to a young man who sat near by; who then came forward, and taking a seat by her side, offered his protection. But made himself so familiar as to excite her fears, rather than comfort her. When the train stopped at the refreshment rooms, he invited her to alight with him, and take some refreshment, but she declined. And while he was absent, another young man came and took possession of his seat, and cautioned her against him, telling her he was a "*black leg.*" She did not know what this expression meant, but supposed it meant something bad. And was inclined to have more confidence in the young man who last took the seat beside her.—But the other soon returned, and claimed his seat. The contention for the seat rose so high, that an elderly gentleman interfered, and said to them, "for the sake of the young woman's feelings, I would say no more about it at this time." The young man who last took the seat, then commended her to the care of this elderly gentleman. She then confidingly looked to him for protection; and he did indeed prove himself worthy her confidence. When they arrived in the city, he conducted her to a hotel, and invited her to take supper, but she could not eat; had not eaten that day. He also made efforts to find her mother, by examining the directory, &c. but without success.

What could she do? a stranger in a strange city; without money enough to support her a day; dressed in the peculiar style of sixty years ago, attracting by her curious habiliments the gaze and wonder of all, timid as a newly caged bird; one hundred and fifty miles from her only earthly home, a home endeared to her by youthful associations and friendships, but from which she had that morning been rashly and most cruelly ejected by those alone to whom she had any right to look (according to her education) for protection and support. She knew she *could* not return to that home. She knew there was no mercy for her there. She had no money to pay her passage back even in the second class cars, or to support her where she was; she had no friends to whom she could look in the world.

This was her condition. Overpowered by the thought of it, she retired to her room for the night. But not taking the precaution immediately to fasten her door, she was directly followed by a scoundrel in the form of a young man, who made insulting advances to her. Her condition was dreadful! but by threats and entreaties he was prevailed on to withdraw, and she immediately fastened her door, and remained alone through the night.

In the morning her friend and protector, the elderly gentleman, again appeared, much to her relief and comfort. She desired to return to Pittsfield. He accordingly put her on board the cars for that place, and generously paid her fare. When she arrived at Pittsfield, she found friends in the anti Shakers there, and soon obtained employment, and was comfortably situated.

She very much regretted that she had forgotten the name of her friend and benefactor, the elderly gentleman. She thought he belonged in Albany, and was a justice of the peace. Should this meet the eye of that gentleman, he may be assured that she appreciated his kindness, and when speaking of him expressed much gratitude. And in behalf of all her friends and for myself, I hereby tender him my lively gratitude.

This case is perhaps rather a strong specimen of their treatment of the young people subject to their power. But this case came under my observation, and I have stated only the literal facts. It is but some of the natural fruits of the system. The doctrine is "crucify the natural affections." And the government is an absolute monarchy. Now it is not strange that those without natural affection, should treat those in their power with cruelty; as they did in the case of this young woman. I say then, her case so far as it goes, is a fair illustration of Shakerism.

In many instances the young people in the society have relations and friends in the vicinity, to whom they can flee for protection. In all such cases they are treated very differently from the case of J. Ann. There have been several instances since she left, in which young sisters have withdrawn from the same Shaker family, and have received from 30 to 40 dollars each as a gift. As they are very careful not to acknowledge any obligation to pay wages. They gave one young man who was in his minority 20 dollars; and his brother who was in his seniority 100 dollars, as I was at first informed.—I have since received from the one who gave me this information, the following correction. "I have since ascertained that R—— did not get but fifty-six dollars, instead of one hundred. He was ashamed to tell me how he had settled. Pretended that he had got his hundred dollars, or they had agreed to give him that. But come to find out, the way they settled it, was this. He told them, he thought he ought to have one hundred dollars; and they pretending to think that about right, got him to sign an acquittance with them of all further claims; which writing however did not state what he was to receive. R—— did not perceive this fraud at the time. They then gave him fifty six dollars, a part in money, and the rest in calfskins out of the tanhouse; and told him if they ever thought he deserved any more, they would give it to him."

It is a common practice of the Shakers when they are about to send or carry off any of the younger members, whom they can no longer control, to lock them up in the office or other out buildings, or place keepers over them until they can carry or send them off. One object of this is probably to prevent any interviews which they might have with their companions. They extremely fear and dread the influence of those who have withdrawn from them. And every means in their power is used to prejudice those who remain against those who have turned off; and to fortify themselves against their influence. "Turn offs," as they are called, are not allowed to visit "Believers," unless there is some particular reason for it.

Intercourse of the Sexes.

It is impossible for young people to crucify all the natural affections. And although all private intercourse between the brethren and sisters is strictly forbidden, and every guard that possibly can be, is placed in the way of it; yet the young brethren and sisters will steal private interviews, fall in love, and go off to the world. During the last part of the time we were there, my wife having the confidence of some of the young sisters, they unbosomed to her many of their trials and adventures on this point. There were but two *young* men in the family, except a few transient comers. The younger was still in his minority, and no less than two of the young sisters had at different times fallen in love with him, and he had had a regular courtship with them, and a regular dissolution of their connexion, or giving up of their meetings. I mean by a regular courtship, that they privately met together by agreement for a considerable length of time, from a regard they had for each other above a common friendship. It must be something more than a common friendship which would induce a sister to break over all the restraints there placed in her way, and continue private meetings with one of the other sex. Meetings of this kind were usually held in the lower hall of the house in the evening, when all the family were above. The parties would take up such a position that if any one came down unexpectedly, they could silently disappear in different directions; and could easily secrete themselves in some of the rooms in this part of the house. Nevertheless, with the greatest caution, detection could not always be avoided. More than one sister also fell in love with the other young brother.

I have room to give only a single specimen on this point. The case occurred in the Church family. I will give the literal facts of the case as briefly as possible, merely changing the names of my young hero and heroine. I make this change not because there is any thing reprehensible in their conduct in the affair, or which should cause them a blush of mortification. But lest there should be a delicacy on their part to having their names made so public in the matter. Those who are already acquainted with the affair will not need the names. With those who are not, the change of names will neither increase nor diminish the interest. The facts are literal; the case not exaggerated.

Story of Mary Williams and William Wright.

Mary Williams was taken to the church family in the "City of Peace" by the consent of her parents, in her early childhood; and grew up to womanhood under the strictest discipline, and all the peculiar instructions and influences of Shakerism. William Wright was also reared in the same family from early childhood, and with equal diligence, with a view to make him a good Believer. Here they grew up, not together exactly, for the two sexes are as carefully kept distinct and separate in childhood, as in youth or adult age. It was only in the meeting room that William could look upon the sweet faces of the little sisterhood, at the farthest extremity from himself, or an occasional glimpse as they glided along the walks of the capacious yards around the dwelling.

As William grew towards manhood, there was one countenance among the young sisters which peculiarly interested him. He could not look upon the face of Mary without pleasurable emotions and a desire to be near and speak to her. But this the regulations of the family did not allow. He had sometimes caught the eye of Mary resting upon himself; this would cause him a momentary thrill of pleasure, and almost create a hope that she had feelings towards him, like those which seemed to chain his own thoughts to her. But then he might not indulge such thoughts and feelings. They were the promptings "of this old carnal nater,"—the very source of all sin and misery. All such feelings he had been taught must be crucified, and his thoughts confessed to his keeper or "caretaker." And Mary he believed must be more innocent, and more faithful to this way and work than himself. And some how or other he could not bring himself to tell his feelings on this subject to his caretakers, but struggled on alone with them. He could not feel that they were sinful in the sight of God.

When about sixteen years of age, the natural good sense and intelligence of Willam's mind had so far mastered the flummeries, and superstitions, forced upon him by education, that he broke his chains and went to the wicked world. But not to stay long away this time. The lovely image of Mary, had been deeply impressed on his heart. She was uppermost in all his thoughts; it was in vain he tried to divert his thoughts from her. He reflected, how unwise he had been to go away from his home and from Mary. By going away he had relinquished all claim to that home. And in all probability Mary would remain, and he could never see her again. The thought was terrible.

Yet there was one ray of hope. Although it was now their rule not to grant any one " a second privilege," yet by humble entreaty, and promises of obedience, the elders might be induced to consider his youth, and receive him back again. He would try. There was also another rule or order, of Shakerism, which was in his favor. It was that every one must regain their union where they lost it. This, if he was received at all, would take him back to the church family. And he would be near his Mary.

With this poor hope William came back. And after many *tearful* entreaties, and humiliations on his part, much delay, and reluctance, on the part of the elders; it was finally decided that he might have another privilege. But great was his chagrin and disappointment when instead of sending him to the church, they put him to the second family. For as to seeing Mary, while he remained in this family, it was no more probable than if he were a hundred miles off. The church family did not meet with the other families for worship, even on the Sabbath. And the young sisters were kept as close as the members of a convent. This was really discouraging; and Shakerism appeared more unlovely than ever. A few months only closed his second privilege.

How William managed his affair, I know not exactly; I can state only what I know. A few days only after he left his second privilege, he boldly rode up to the church-house with a horse and carriage, and carried away his natural sister who was a member of that family. As she was ready to go with him, it seems there must have been some concert between them; but by what means it would be difficult to divine. A few months after this, young William might have been seen cautiously passing through the Shaker village, and circuitously making his way to one of the out-buildings, a short distance from the families dwelling. This building was employed as a workshop by the sisters; and was unoccupied through the night. In this building Mary had for a considerable length of time held clandestine meetings with William, during the silent "watches of the night." She was always accompanied in these visits by her companion and bedmate. But as the saying is, " true love never runs smooth." So in the case of poor William; by some means, the thing had come to the knowledge of the elders. The two sisters concerned in this affair, were hauled up before their confessors, and obliged to unfold the whole affair. Their position was such that they could do no otherwise.

They did not of course arise that night to meet the loving swain. But young William, suspecting no mischief, but revolving those pleasurable, anticipations which true love alone can inspire, came to the place of meeting and gave the usual signal upon the door; it being answered from within as had been agreed upon, he boldly went in. Then imagine his surprise, when advancing as he supposed to take his beloved Mary affectionately by the hand, there stood before him, instead of his Mary, and her companion, *Sister Dana*, of the ministry, and the *second eldress* of the church family. And turning to flee from these high functionaries, behold, there stood between him and the closed door, Joseph Wicker, and Simon Maybee, the second elder and deacon of the church family. He was their prisoner, and there was no escape. He doubtless felt the *awkwardness*, if not the danger, of his position. It is said they compelled the poor fellow to make all the confessions and promises they desired. They, the elder, and deacon, then politely escorted him to the outskirts of the village, and permitted him to depart. And as he left them he politely thanked them for their attentions. Mary and her companion shortly after, notwithstanding their confessions and humiliations, were cruelly driven from their home, to find an asylum in the wicked world.

As a further relation of this case has no direct reference to the subject on whose account it has been quoted, I will here drop it. These little love adventures are continually occurring, all over the Shaker kingdom, where there are young men and women, with those affections with which God has wisely endowed the race of mankind. The natures which God has given us are stronger than the chains of superstition, and priestcraft.

But the world is curious to know what is the practice of the elder members of the Shaker community on this subject. It is already well known that the doctrine they teach, is, *total abstinence from all indulgence of the flesh.* All indulgence of the flesh, is sinful. This is *the* fundamental doctrine of the denomination. It is also very generally believed in the world that the Shakers do not practice the doctrine they preach, but are very corrupt on this point. Especially the Lead. I would gladly abstain from speaking on this point, if my duty would allow of it. Having had two years experience among them, the public will not excuse me, if I do not give my testimony on the subject.

This I will endeavor to do with all candor and impartiality. In the first place then, I will say very distinctly, and cheerfully, that I have no *proof* that they do not live up to the doctrine on this point. I am fully persuaded that a very large portion of the common members are honest in their belief of this doctrine, and faithful in its practice, if indeed, I may judge other families by the one in which I resided. An intimate connexion of two years with this family enables me to speak confidently on this point. The delinquencies of which I have spoken among the young people are not chargeable upon the Lead. For they do all in their power to prevent. So far all is consistent.

Are the Ministry and Elders Pure?

But the grand question is, are the ministry and elders pure? is their practice in accordance with their professions? It is well known that some who have withdrawn from the Shakers, have boldly charged the Lead with excessive licentiousness of the flesh. Mary Dyer seems to have proved such charges by good testimony. This must pass for what it is worth. Not being personally acquainted with her, or her witnesses, I am not competent fully to appreciate her proof. I also saw and read the reply to her book by the Shakers, in the name of her husband, Joseph Dyer, who, with some or all of the children, remained with the Shakers. This also seemed to be composed of good testimony. It is many years since I saw Mary Dyer's book, and I can hardly pretend to remember much about it, except the charge of drunkenness, and licentiousness, against the ministry, and elders. And that she had a large mass of testimony to prove these charges.

In regard to the reply to this book by the Shakers, in the name of Joseph Dyer; there is one very great objection to it. It is this. The witnesses made to testify in that case in behalf of the Shakers, are *interested* witnesses. They testify for their "*Lead*," the ministry and elders. They are subject to this *lead* in all respects; dependent on this *Lead* for all things. The doctrine continually and zealously inculcated throughout Shakerdom, is, that obedience, a childlike obedience to the Lead, is necessary to a union with Believers here, and to their eternal salvation. And it is very well known by all who are at all acquainted with this people, that those who do not live in obedience to the Lead, cannot remain with that people. But are driven from home, and friends, pennyless to the world.

Every motive, therefore, which heaven, and earth can afford, may, by the ministry, and elders, be brought to bear on these witnesses, to compel them to testify as the Lead desire. Their testimony, therefore, cannot when duly considered, have much, if any, weight in the case. It would be *wholly* inadmissible in any legal cause. In which case, Mary Dyer's book would be considered as unanswered. But leaving this part of the evidence for the present, let us proceed to inquire what other evidence there is in the case.

As I before stated, in my two years experience there, I

obtained no proof that the Lead were guilty of a criminal indulgence of the flesh, yet, I cannot speak so positively of their innocence, as I have of that of the common members. In the first place, they are men, and women, with the same affections, and passions, as other men, and women. In the second place, if they are disposed to indulge the " carnal nature," they can do so, and defy detection. The beloved ministry of each diocese, composed of two males, and two females, have their dwelling in the upper part of the meeting-house. Their retirement here is sacred. No one is permitted to call on them there, not even the elders. Whenever the elders call on them, it must be at their shops, or work-houses. There may be, and probably are cases of exception to this rule. In case of extreme illness, or death, they call in assistance from the church. But they always take care of each other when they can. The rule, or order, is, that none but the elders shall call on the ministry, at all. Here then, is every opportunity, and all the natural inclinations on the one hand, and their professions of celibacy from religious principle on the other. And they have unlimited authority over all the other members of their Diocese. This is their position. And people who form their opinion from these facts alone, will come to very different conclusions. If they sincerely and devoutly believe the system of religion they teach, it *may* have power to restrain them in a majority of cases. But if it should in all cases, it would be truly miraculous. We have as much reason, to say the least of it, to believe in the sincerity of the Roman Catholic Priesthood, as in that of the Shaker Priesthood. And their corruption in this respect is too notorious to be denied. And there are a *few* cases in which Protestant Clergymen have been proved to be basely corrupt in the flesh. But I will leave every one to draw his own conclusions in this matter.

The position of the elders, though not exactly like that of the ministry, is very similar to it. The two elders and two eldresses of every family in the denomination, (in some instances there is but one elder and two eldresses) have their private meetings, or meetings by themselves, three evenings in every week. They have their private apartments, and as much secrecy as they may choose. And although the holy laws declare expressly that "a brother and sister shall not be together in a room by themselves alone, with the door closed. And the brethren shall not go into the sister's rooms, or the sisters into the brethren's without knocking, and being bid to come in." It is stated in connexion that "These laws are not designed to apply to the elders."

It may not be inappropriate to repeat here, one fact which I have before stated. Althought hese laws and orders profess to be given by special inspiration, they are submitted to the "Lord's Anointed," the ministry and elders; to be enforced *if* they approve of them. To be repeated, altered or amended according to their *wisdom.* "The wisdom with which I have annointed them saith the Lord." Extensive blanks are left in the record of these laws, to be filled up by the ministry according to their wisdom. And I remember very well that at the close of the record, it is said, "If the blessed ministry approve of these laws, they may affix their names to them." I may not have quoted the language verbatim, but I have quoted the idea.

I make these quotations to show that the ministry and elders are above the laws; and all their submission to them, must in the nature of the case, be a voluntary submission. Those very laws and orders which form the barriers to the sexual intercourse of the common members, are declared in the text not to apply to the elders. This fact was very ominous to my mind. Though doubtless the ostensible reason of this indulgence to the elders was, and it would abundantly satisfy the good believer, that it was given them that they might the better watch over and protect their subjects.

With one or two remarks I will submit this case without expressing my own opinion If the mass of the Shakers were guilty of indulging the flesh, their guilt would be notorious to the world. It could not in the nature of things be hid. The Lead are aware of this, and it is their first object to guard and protect them against such indulgences. On the other hand, if the *few* only, who have the absolute control of all things there, are disposed to indulge, even if they now and then select an instrument from the common members, they would seldom be liable to exposure.

In consideration therefore of all the facts and circumstances of the case, the affections and passions which the Lead have in common with other men, and their opportunity to indulge them, is it probable, regardless of the charges which others, more nearly connected with them than I have been, have brought against them, and seem to have sustained by good testimony; is it probable I say, regardless of these charges and testimony, that the Lead do live a life of celibacy?

Believing as I do, and as I think the facts set forth in this work clearly show, that Shakerism is (principally at least) a game which the Lead perpetrate upon the common members, it would not be thought strange if I should make up my mind against them. Nevertheless, the kindness and liberality extended to me and mine while among them, lead me to cherish a more charitable hope. The fact that they endeavored to dupe me in common with others is of but little consequence, as I had the satisfaction of telling them when I left, that I so far understood the game, that it was impossible it should ever succeed with me; and the principles of it were of such a nature, that I could not conscientiously act an intelligent part in carrying them out.

There were two cases of foundling children while I was there. The first was that of a male infant, supposed to be about three weeks old. It was found on Sabbath morning, in one of the buildings of the West family, carefully packed in a willow basket, and left in the wagon used by the family to ride to meeting. They made some efforts to discover the parents of the child, but without success. As there had been a slight fall of rain the night previous, and no carriages had been seen to pass through the village that morning, they were enabled to trace the marks of a horse and carriage which seemed to have come from the way of New Lebanon, and returned again in that direction. David Terry, who has the care of this family, also went out into Pittsfield, and made some inquiries of a woman, of whose daughter they had some suspicions. She told him that in all probability the mother of the child was much nearer his home than that place. They gave the child over to the authorities of the town.

The other was that of a boy, supposed to be about two years old. He was found standing upon the doorsteps of the house of the church family, not very late in the evening. This case was advertised and a reward of twenty dollars offered for the discovery of the parents. It was remarked however, by good believers, that this was done for appearance's sake, as they did not wish to be rid of the child. The elder of the family adopted him, and manifested an extreme fondness for him. His fondness for the child was remarked throughout the village.

A brief notice of some of their principal doctrines.

The doctrine of celibacy, considered abstractly, is not so very objectionable. Every one has a right to practice it who chooses to, or feels it a duty to, provided he can keep himself virtuous; but every means of unnatural gratification of sexual desires, is injurious, and sinful. But this is not the principal objection to the Shaker doctrine of celibacy. "The cross," as they express it, requires that all "*the natural affections*" be crucified. Parental and filial affection, and all love of natural relations, is as contrary to the doctrine of the cross as conjugal love. It is all carnal and must be put away. To overcome and extinguish all the natural affections, is the great end of the Shaker life. To do this, is the taking up of "the cross against the world, flesh and devil," which is necessary to a life of purity, and to salvation.

Suppose then this doctrine to be carried into full and practical effect. What is a man without "natural affections?" The apostle in the first chapter of his epistle to the Romans, classes those "without natural affections," with the worst of criminals; as murderers, haters of God, &c. And I hold that such would be the character of all who might succeed in crucifying to extinction the natural affections. If this were thoroughly accomplished, there would be no goodness left. Love is the very element of all goodness. There can be no goodness which does not flow from this element. And love is a unit. Always of the same nature. It exhibits itself in different degrees; and is qualified only by the objects upon which it is exercised. Parental, filial, conjugal, natural and spiritual love, are but different modifications or directions of the same thing. "He who saith I love God, and loveth not his brother, is a liar, and the truth is not in him. For if he love not his brother whom he hath seen, how can he love God whom he hath not seen?" And it is but a slight extension of this saying of the apostle, to apply it to our natural relations. It is even more manifest that he who does not love his own natural brother, or his children and near relations, cannot love God. There is no love in his heart. He has not the element of goodness about him. This is the natural and necessary result of the Shaker doctrine, if it could be practically and fully carried out. But it cannot; they have in common with other people a large share of the element of goodness left.

But they teach that we should love all, with that fraternal love which christianity requires. We all agree that it is our duty to cherish love to all as the children of God, and heirs of an immortal inheritance. But we do not agree that it would be right to love our children less than we do. And a command of God is, "Husbands, love your wives." This does not imply that we should crucify or shake off the "natural affections."

Indeed, this doctrine is so manifestly absurd as hardly to deserve a serious consideration. It is not so much a conviction of the truth of this doctrine that sustains Shakerism, as belief in their pretended revelations. It seems to me a mere statement of the doctrine is sufficient. And this I have given. It is clearly a duty rather than a sin, for parents to love their children. And if a duty to love and provide for them, it is no sin to beget and have them. But I drop the subject, fully believing this Shaker doctrine false and untenable. And that they are living in an unnatural and false position. A position unfavorable to the developement of the faculties and energies of the soul or mind, and body. And unfavorable to true happiness, temporal and spiritual.

The Second Advent.

On this subject, I shall make but one or two brief remarks. It seems to me that they cannot expect the doctrine that Ann Lee was the second appearance of Christ, to gain extensive credence. The minister of this society told me, that if a man believed in taking up his cross against the flesh, he did not care whether he believed their doctrine of the second advent or not. Still this is a fundamental doctrine of Shakerism. Mother Ann was, (nominally at least) the founder of the sect. If her pretensions were false, so are the pretensions of her followers. If she was not inspired, they are not inspired. If she was not anointed of God, so are they not anointed. Their inspirations, revelations, laws and orders are all a mere sham, and a pretence. A game played upon the unsuspecting.

Her followers of course must believe that she was all she pretended to be. But in the world she has the reputation of being, and there is much testimony to show that she was, an immoral woman. Intemperate, licentious, and passionate. It is testified by some who were intimate with her that she has been seen to strike the elders in anger, &c. It was testified by some of the most respectable people who lived near the Shakers in her day, that they had frequently seen her intoxicated. And on one occasion she was seen vomiting from drunkenness. An explanation was afterwards given by one of her followers. It was, that " she was drunk, not with liquor, but with the sins of the people; which she was vomiting up." In those days intemperance was not regarded as it now is. And the Shakers made a free use of intoxicating beverages. And not until long since the commencement of the temperance reform, did the Lord in his wisdom see fit to send them instructions, or laws, curtailing the use of such beverages. And even now the ministry and elders use them in the form of cordials and bitters; and sometimes without such disguises, but privately. A quart of cider a day, on week days, is allowed to some of the common members who are unwilling to do without it. No doubt then, " Mother and the elders with her," used intoxicating drinks. But to what excess we know not.

I have before me a work on Shakerism, by William J. Haskett, formerly a member of the society. This work was printed in 1828, and is entitled " Shakerism unmasked." This author treats the society with much charity and candor. He believes the Shakers sincere, though a *deluded* people. This is doubtless true of the mass of them. But when we look at the subject, with a view to investigate the facts, it at once appears impossible, that such a stupendous fraud could be carried on sixty years, by men blindfolded. The perfect system, by which every thing is managed, all the details of their government, and all their religious flummery and mummery; and all by express revelation. How they can manage to have every thing revealed, just to suit their purposes, and not have it revealed, nor intelligently plan it themselves, is a riddle too deep for common minds. A miracle as great as any the Shakers pretend to. Since brother Hasket has renounced Shakerism, and still believes in the sincerity of the Lead, he should have explained this point.—He says, on page 148, of his book, when speaking of the ministry, " They make all the orders and gifts, and declare them to have been given by divine revelation. And as such, enforce them on the members." On page 184, he says, " The Shakers declare that each, and every one of them, was given by divine revelation, and came from God." Now these statements, I know, are true. But in view of them, how can we believe in the sincerity of those who frame them? Here is a design and a purpose in view; and it requires thought, intelligence, and deliberation to meet the case. To frame the laws and orders of an extensive government; but, professedly, they are all given by specia revelation.—And then all the great "Gifts," such as the gift of the "Father and Son;" The "Gift of Holy Mother Wisdom;" The "cleansing Gift," &c. &c. All evidently framed with a design to effect an object; are also made by the ministry, and universally adopted, and carried out by the families throughout the denomination.—And then the use made of confessions. The common members suppose, that when their confessions are made to the elders, their sins confessed, are blotted out in heaven, and this with them is the end of the matter. They know not that they are carried up to the ministry; but so it is. And by this means the ministry learn the condition of their people, and frame for them such *laws* and *gifts*, as their condition is supposed to require. And yet all this is by revelation, and comes from God. The common members generally believe so. But to admit that the ministry believe it, is giving their hearts very great credit; but at the expense of their intelligence. There is, however, no doubt of their intelligence.

Mr. Haskett also quotes from Mr. Brown's history of the Shakers, in which he (Mr. Brown) observes, that this principle was inculcated by the first elders, in the following words, "That no practice is wrong, nor oath false, which is made to gain the cause of truth, or defend the gospel against error, though it might appear directly opposite to truth, in the eyes of the world, yet as done for the cause of the gospel, it is considered as true."

I have heard denials made by the elders, and ministry, for which I could not account on any other principle.—In saying that the "Lead" manage this system of Shakerism by means of deception, or that Shakerism is a fraud practiced on the common members by the Lead, it is but just and proper that I should make some qualification. There is no system of religion wholly erroneous. Shakerism has much in it that is true and excellent. But whatever characterises it, whatever is peculiar to it, is chiefly, if not wholly erroneous. And these are the things which I wish to place before the public, and have noticed in this work. Probably there are none, even among the Lead, but what believe some of the things which belong to the system. They may all believe for aught I know, that it is a duty to take up their "cross" against the flesh. It is not necessary to any practical purpose to decide this point. The only question which I care to decide, as touching their sincerity, is, Do they believe their pretended revelations? I will divide this question into several. 1st, Do the ministry and elders sincerely and devotedly believe, that the " *Turning* " (as it is called) by the brethren and sisters, is by a supernatural or miraculous power, a special gift of God? or do they perform this *turning* by their own natural powers, rendered more active by the excitement of the occasion? This turning is commonly practiced in all their most *lively* meetings. It is more common among the young sisters, than any other portion of the members. It is merely turning the body around from right to left, or from left to right, with different degrees of rapidity; in some instances I should judge, near sixty times in a minute. And varying in time, from a few minutes to an hour.

The family elder, acknowledged to me, on this subject, that he did not believe every thing of this kind, was by special inspiration. " Perhaps nine tenths of the turning by the young brethren and sisters was *of* themselves." What proof then, is there, that the other one tenth is supernatural, than there is that the nine tenths is. And there is no more proof that this turning among the Sbakers, is by a supernatural power, than there is that the turning by those Anti-Shakers who have exhibited about the country, is by a supernatural power. It is said, practice makes perfect. Practice has a great deal to do with this Gift of turning. Those who can turn in Shaker meeting, can turn any where else. Though the excitement of the meeting, doubtless, increases their ability.

2d, Do the ministry and elders sincerely and devotedly believe, that the sputtering or gibberish which we hear, mostly from the sisters, in very exciting meetings, or what is commonly called among them " unknown," is really any language which was ever spoken on earth or in heaven? and is it by any special gift of God, that they thus speak?—There are some among the Shakers who can speak German or Dutch; and some who can speak French, having learned the same. I do not allude to such, but to those who pretend to speak an unknown language, by the special gift of God.

3d. Do the ministry and elders sincerely and devotedly believe that all the laws and orders by which the society is governed, are given by the special inspiration of God?

These questions relate to the very pillars upon which the whole fabric or system of Shakerism rests. Let the Lead renounce their belief in these things, and in a very short time there would be a division of the property. Their whole authority and power rests on the belief of the society in the *divinity* of these things.

On the other hand, if the Lead can truly and honestly answer the foregoing questions in the affirmative, we must admit that they are honest, but deluded men. But it is impossible; they cannot be so much deluded. And all the excuse they can make to their consciences, for the part they act, must be, that they are deceiving the common members for their good.—It is possible that some of the family elders may believe these things, and at the same time be instrumental in carrying on the game. But in the very nature of things, the greater part must act intelligently.

This is a subject of very great importance. Many of the noblest hearts, the most disinterested philanthropists of this world, in their dreams of a state of society, in which all the good things which may be enjoyed in this world, should be equally enjoyed by the members composing it; have dwelt much upon the idea of a common property. Others have endeavored to obtain the benefits which a common property might be supposed to afford, without directly adopting the principle. By creating a community of interest, by means of joining their capital stock in company, but maintaining their claim to it in certificates, or other writings. Many societies or communities have been formed from time to time, adopting the principle of a community, the community of Rapp, and of Bindler, of the Owenists, the Fourierists, &c.

I think it may be said of these communities, that none of them have realized the grand object aimed in their organization. Many of these have failed entirely ; others are on the decline, and all of them probably find dificulties and trials, which will more than balance the good acquired. The Shakers have by means of their absolute monarchy, the power of their religion being made to bear also on this point, and a covenant by which the members consecrate all their property and labor to the society, accumulated great wealth. And by similar means the communities of Rapp and Bindler have become rich.—But the multitudes who have seceded from the Shakers, after having signed the covenant, have by this means been stripped of all they possessed. It is in a great measure, by this (though legally honest yet morally dishonest) means that the Shakers have acquired much of their wealth.—And notwithstanding their wealth, they are, as a denomination, on the decline. Their secessions are many more than their accessions. And a very large proportion of their members are superannuated The young people secede ; the old remain.

Their government is a tyranny, its subjects are in bondage. The community of property, was undoubtedly adopted " in the first of the faith," in the very strongest Christian love. In process of time, and not a very long time, their unjust covenant became a matter of necessity to protect the community property. The demands of seceders (secessions were, and always have been, numerous,) was likely to carry it all away.

And here I apprehend is one grand difficulty, in all communities of interest as well as of property. If the property may be withdrawn at the option of the communitist, the business and objects of the community are embarrassed by it, and ultimately defeated. If bound permanently, or for a long time, the rights, and liberties, of the members are encroached upon. For, although the relinquishment of property, or claims for labor, is voluntary at the time, it is none the less by a forced submission when the member has changed his mind. And if held against his will, he becomes unfriendly to the enterprise. And in process of time, internal enemies of the community prove its ruin. As I have spoken of the Shaker covenant as unjust, I will here, for the want of the covenant itself, quote the substance of it as given by William J. Haskett, which is doubtless correct.

"And we do by these presents solemnly covenant with each other, for ourselves, and assigns, never hereafter, to bring debt, or demand against the said deacons, nor their successors, nor against any member of the church, or community, jointly, or severally, on account of our services, or property, thus devoted and consecrated to the aforesaid sacred and charitable uses." "And we also covenant with each other, to subject ourselves in union, as brethren and sisters, who are called to follow Christ, in regeneration, in obedience to the order, rules, and government of church. And this covenant shall be a sufficient witness for us before all men, and in all cases relating to the possession, order, and use, of the joint interest of the church. In testimony whereof, we have, both brethren and sisters, hereunto subscribed our names, in presence of each other, this twenty-fourth day of June, in the year of our Lord one thousand eight hundred and one."

By virtue of this covenant the trustees have the power to dispose and manage the property according to their wisdom, with the approval of the ministry, and for the good of the society. But the ministry have power to appoint, depose, and re-appoint these trustees, or deacons, according to their own pleasure, or caprice. So the whole concern is under the entire control of the ministry. If the ministry are disposed to give a seceder any thing, they can so do; otherwise they must go pennyless. There have been many cases recently, in which some females have received from thirty to forty dollars. And some young brethren from twenty to a hundred dollars. But in such cases they must withdraw very quietly, pledge themselves not to injure the society, by signing a sort of quitclaim, and receive the money as a present. In a great majority of cases the amount received is merely nominal.

Some of the principal difficulties in the way of communities may be very briefly stated. The one mentioned above is insuperable. It is impossible to accumulate and retain permanently a sufficient amount of property, for the success of a large community, without encroaching upon the rights, and privileges of individuals, as in the case of the Shakers, and all communities of common property. Individuals are robbed, or enslaved by means of the organization. The restraints, and subordination necessary to the order, harmony and success of a compact community, are unnatural and intolerable to those who love freedom. And consequently secessions are and must be in the nature of things frequent. And save those in authority and their favorites, the seceders are the freest spirits, the life and energy of the community. And this indicates an important fact, viz., that a compact community is not a desirable state of society. And also that it is inconsistent with freedom. The Shakers, becoming aware of this fact by experiment, take every means in their power to suppress intelligence, promote superstition, and thus create a superstitious fear, secure all the property, and by these means joined with their despotism, as a community they have dragged out an existence of nearly sixty years. But the community is now in spite of all these means on the decline.

But suppose a community could be established with ample property, and members of the right sort. The natural indolence of mankind would form a great objection to their success. Men will not act without motive; and will not act with energy without a strong motive. In such a community, the chief care and responsibility of the concern, must in the nature of the case devolve upon the few. The mass being directed in their labors, the support of themselves and families being provided for by the organization; they have little comparatively to call forth, or at least to force into action the energies of their minds. If the community go on harmoniously, they will naturally settle down in this security, and grow mentally indolent.

This fact has a very full illustration among the Shakers. Those who have settled down for life, that is, with a full and settled determination to be good " Believers," have no care, or anxiety about this life. And it is painfully disgusting to see with what a willing servility they conform to all the elders require of them, and go through with all the silly and childish performances carried out in their meetings. On these things they suppose their salvation to depend, and this being secured by obedience, their thoughts do not seem to extend beyond these trivial matters.

In a community on the principles of Fourier, there would be more to exercise and call forth the energies of the mind; but even here, it would be found that Fourier's emulation by means of groups, and series, music and pleasurable amusements, though they might operate well for a season, the generation *succeeding* the founders of the community, to say the least, would be very little affected by them; and they would fail to counteract in the mass, the natural indolence of mankind. Vice, and imbecility, are the natural fruits of a dormant mind. The mass of the Shakers are protected against actual vice by the inquisition of their government, and a superstitious fear.

In the present condition of the human mind, the cares, and anxieties, as well as the affections of domestic life, are necessary to the full developement of *the man*. He cannot arrive at his full stature as a man until these things call forth his hidden energies. And he must feel that his beloved ones are liable to poverty, and the other evils incident to this life, and that it is his duty, and his glory to protect and guard them against these evils. These things alone are sufficient to develope all the energies of the human mind, and character, in its present condition. True, some minds, naturally active, need not the most powerful motives in order to exert themselves.

Those who are the most zealous to reorganize society, would do well to bestow much thought upon this subject. Especially the advocates, if there are any, of common property. There is perhaps no good reason why congenial minds should not draw near each other in neighborhoods;

sympathise with, and assist each other in the trials and difficulties of life, and co-operate in benevolent objects. But a more compact community which seeks to bind itself by a common property, or any means which shall encroach upon the independence of individuals, or individual interests of its members, will be found to be attended with more evils than benefits.

Let the intellect be improved, all the natural affections cultivated, purified, and enlarged, both social and domestic, and society will improve its organization as a consequence. No radical improvement can be effected on any other foundation. There is much error, tyranny, and corruption, in the present organization of society, both in its civil and religious departments. But the spirit of reform is abroad; intelligence and love will accomplish wonderful things.

My experience among the Shakers taught me not only that that people were corrupt and deluded, but also confirmed my former opinion, that creeds, and covenants are dangerous, and injurious to the progress of society. They are adopted on the ground that our present opinions are infallible, and forbid all change; and consequently stand in the way of improvement. It is a fact which is confirmed by all history that all those organizations which are bound by creeds, and covenants, and have party interests to promote, are the greatest obstacles in the way of moral reform. Every reform, from the temperance reform, to the peace movement, have been obliged in the outset, to combat all such organizations. Let no man then bow down to another man's opinion, or bind himself by any creed, or covenant, so that he will not be at liberty to embrace and carry out any new light, or reform, which the progress of the world may develope. Maintain your own liberty of opinion, and your own right to do good in your own way.